D0668199

THE RUDE AWAKENING

HOW SAVED ARE WE?

Other Books by Michael L. Brown

From Holy Laughter to Holy Fire:
America on the Edge of Revival

Israel's Divine Healer
(Studies in Old Testament Biblical Theology)

It's Time to Rock the Boat:
A Call to God's People to Rise Up
and Preach a Confrontational Gospel

Our Hands Are Stained With Blood:
The Tragic Story of the "Church" and the Jewish People

Whatever Happened to the Power of God:
Is the Charismatic Church Slain in the Spirit
or Down for the Count?

The End of the American Gospel Enterprise

Compassionate Father or Consuming Fire?
Who Is the God of the Old Testament?

Let No One Deceive You:
Confronting the Critics of Revival

For information on ICN Ministries, or for a listing of other books and tapes by Michael L. Brown, write to:

ICN Ministries
P.O. Box 36157
Pensacola, FL 32506
Phone: (850) 458-6424
FAX: (850) 458-1828
E-mail: RevivalNow@msn.com

THE RUDE AWAKENING

HOW SAVED ARE WE?

BY

MICHAEL L. BROWN

Dedicated to the memory of Michael W. Block

Destiny Image® Publishers, Inc.
P.O. Box 310
Shippensburg, PA 17257-0310

"Speaking to the Purposes of God for This Generation
and for the Generations to Come"

ISBN 1-56043-055-9

For Worldwide Distribution
Printed in the U.S.A.

Fourth Printing: 1996   Fifth Printing: 1997

This book and all other Destiny Image, Revival Press,
and Treasure House books are available
at Christian bookstores and distributors worldwide.

For a U.S. bookstore nearest you, call **1-800-722-6774**.
For more information on foreign distributors, call **717-532-3040**.
Or reach us on the Internet: **http://www.reapernet.com**

Contents

Preface

The words of this book have not been written lightly. They are the result of much soul searching and rending of heart. They have caused me to ask some unsettling questions: How far have we fallen from the New Testament faith? Do we really understand what it means to be saved?

It is disturbing to hear so many believers talk about their churches and their personal lives as if everything was wonderful, as if they were experiencing the fullness of the Spirit, as if they were living as true disciples of the Lord. The plain truth is that we hardly know how little we have and how little we are accomplishing.

I do not claim to have all the answers. I certainly have not yet "arrived." But this much is absolutely clear: Unless the American Church experiences a radical reformation, we will fade right into the world. We think we are alive and well, but we are really sick and dying. May God awaken us to our true condition before it is too late!

Over the last few years, I have had the joy of working with some missionaries in different parts of the world. Last November, when returning from ten days of ministry with the Christ is the

Answer teams in Italy and Portugal, these thoughts kept rising within me: If *we* — American believers — are saved in the same way *they* are saved, why don't most of us have the same passion for souls that they have? Why have they sacrificed everything to preach the gospel while we often find it hard to sacrifice *anything* to preach the gospel? Isn't the harvest ripe all around us — wherever we are? Isn't the Lord urging us on to sell out and serve Him wholeheartedly right here and right now? Why then are we so complacent? Why are we so at home in a fallen world? Why do we hardly mourn?

This much is apparent: Because our gospel message has been deficient, our disciples are now deficient and the American "born again" Church is deficient. Our lifestyles give little evidence of a real transformation and concepts like sacrifice and suffering for the Lord are almost foreign to us. Even our "thriving" congregations need a radical reorientation. We have heaped up blessings for ourselves in this life but have lost sight of eternity. God is not pleased with all this.

What do we do when the Lord begins to open our eyes? How do we respond to the searching light of His Spirit and His Word? First we must remember that He convicts, challenges and corrects — but He does not condemn. *All of us stand by grace.* He only shows us the problem in order to lead us to the solution. *We need to go back to the basics.* While it is true that we can be instantaneously converted, many of us were never confronted with the real claims of the gospel when we "received the Lord." Are we really following Jesus? Do we even know what this means? Are we willing to be holy radicals — whatever the cost?

Of course I realize that not all of us are called to the foreign missions field, and not all of us can drop everything we are doing and stand on the street corners and preach. But I am sure that wherever we are in this world, God can take hold of us, make us into flames of fire, and use us to shake our society for His glory. Being saved means standing up — and standing out.

For all those who are prompted by the Spirit to get involved with missions giving or missions service, I encourage you to contact the organizations listed at the back of this book.

After I began to write these chapters last December, I was blessed to see some encouraging signs in the air. More and more children of God have realized that something fundamental is wrong, and different voices from different camps have been addressing these very same issues. And both in America as well as overseas, the controversy is swirling regarding "Lordship Salvation." While it is pitiful to hear people try to argue that you can be saved *without* submitting to Jesus as Lord, at least this error is being brought to the light. May the Spirit of truth shine forth!

My thanks again to Michael Murray for carefully and thoughtfully reading the manuscript; to Don Nori and the Destiny Image staff for helping to see this project through; to our fellow workers at Beth Messiah Congregation and Messiah Biblical Institute, for faithful intercession; to our loyal friends in the States and abroad, for all their love and support; to Leonard and Martha Ravenhill, for their passion for the Lord and their prayers for me; and to my wonderful wife Nancy, a special gift from God. She continues to urge me on in the Lord, to yield my all for His glory.

May the Lord Jesus find Himself a people who are hungry for the real thing. To Him alone be the praise!

Michael L. Brown
July, 1990

Chapter One

How Saved Are We?

The American Church at the end of the twentieth century is experiencing a crisis. For years we have preached a cheap gospel and peddled a soft Savior. We have taught salvation without self-denial and the crown without the cross. We have catered to the unsaved and compromised with the world. Now we are paying the price.

Our "instant salvation" message has dishonored God and deluded men. Our faulty seeds have produced a flaky harvest. What a pitiful crop we are reaping!

As American "believers" we:
spend hours watching television but minutes watching in prayer;
are hungry for the sports page but have little taste for the Word;
spend more money on pet food than on foreign missions;
love to feast but hate to fast;
welcome God's blessings but are wary of His burdens.

Is this what Jesus died for? Is this our "new life" in Him?

Stop for a moment and think:
Anyone who spends more time playing video games than seeking God in prayer has no right to call Jesus Lord.

Anyone who takes delight in today's perverted soap operas is serving another god.

Anyone who cannot die to sports for a season is worshiping idols.

"If anyone loves the world, the love of the Father is not in him . . . because friendship with the world is hatred toward God" (1 John 2:15; James 4:4).
In reality, whose friends are we?

It's time for some serious soul searching. What kind of "born again" experience have we had if it calls for almost no personal sacrifice, produces virtually no separation from the world, and breeds practically no hatred of sin? How can we claim to be "born from above"? Where is the evidence of our "new nature"?

We call ourselves "citizens of heaven" — yet our hearts are caught up in earthly treasures. We sing, "We're the people of God" — but we are entertained by the worst of the devil's children. We claim to be "dead to the world" — yet we are more interested in temporal fashions than in eternal souls. Something is wrong with our "salvation" experience! *Bad fruits mean bad roots.*

We say, "Just confess Jesus as Lord and you're in!"
He says, "Not everyone who says to Me, 'Lord, Lord,' will enter the kingdom of heaven, but only *he who does the will of My Father* in heaven" (Matt 7:21).

We say, "Just pray this prayer and it's done!"
He says, "If anyone would come after Me, *he must deny himself and take up his cross daily and follow Me"* (Luke 9:23).

We say, "Just come to the altar. It will only take a minute!"
He says, *"Make every effort to enter through the narrow door,* because many I tell you, will try to enter and will not be able to" (Luke 13:24). Who do you think is right?

Jesus made it painfully clear to the large crowds who were traveling with Him:

"If anyone comes to Me and does not hate his father and mother, his wife and children, his brothers and sisters — yes, even his own life — he *cannot be My disciple*."

"Anyone who does not carry his cross and follow Me *cannot be My disciple*."

"Any of you who does not give up everything he has *cannot be My disciple*" (Luke 14:26,27,33).

Who do we think we're fooling? *It's time to count the cost!*

Maybe we have truly "come to Jesus"; but can we say we are *following* Him? Maybe we have believed the "Good News"; but are we daily carrying our crosses? Jesus commanded us to "go and make disciples of all nations" (Matt. 28:19). Maybe *we* need to become disciples first.

Yes, salvation is "by grace through faith," and we can add nothing to it. But it is the *grace* of God that "teaches us to say 'No' to ungodliness and worldly passions, and to live self-controlled, upright and godly lives in this present age" (Titus 2:11-12). And *true faith* is known by what it does, since "faith without deeds is useless" (James 2:20).

Paul warned the Ephesians not to let anyone deceive them with *empty words*. "Of this you can be sure," he said. "No immoral, impure or greedy person — such a man is an idolater — has *any* inheritance in the kingdom of Christ and of God" (Eph. 5:5). Do we think that God's standard has changed? Do "carnal Christians" go to carnal heaven? No. "Without holiness no one will see the Lord. . . . Those who belong to Christ Jesus have crucified the sinful nature with its passions and desires. . . . *You are not your own;* you were bought with a price. [Only *slaves* were bought with a price.] Therefore honor God with your body" (Heb. 12:14; Gal. 5:24; 1 Cor. 6:19-20). We must come to terms with these words!

Discipleship is not optional. Neither is it cheap. Peter said, Lord, "we have left everything to follow You!" (Mark 10:28). What have *we* left to follow Him? "Every material gift increases its value if it comes not from money you can dispense with, but from the sacrifice of something you would love to have" (Richard Wurmbrand). How much have we *really* given for Him?

Johanna Veenstra went as a single woman missionary to Africa in 1920. She lived in a primitive hut with dirt floors, plagued with white ants and rats. "When having my evening meal," she reported, "here were those [white ants] in swarms, sticking fast in hand, dropping in the food — and I concluded a plague was upon us. There was no 'shutting' them out because in these native huts we have no ceiling." But there were no complaints from her lips; and in spite of very little initial success, she had no second thoughts. "There has never been a single regret that I left the 'bright lights and gay life' of New York City, and came to this dark corner of his vineyard. There has been no sacrifice, because the Lord Jesus Himself is my constant companion."

Like the disciples of old, she was saved.

What about us? How saved are we?

Chapter Two

It's Time To Die!

Crucifixion was one of the most hideous forms of execution ever devised by man. It was the basest of deaths, reserved for slaves and rebels. Cicero called it "the supreme capital penalty, the most painful, dreadful, and ugly." There was no greater suffering or humiliation. The condemned person would usually be scourged until his back was a mass of torn flesh. Then he would be exposed to public mockery, sometimes stripped naked. Then he would be crucified. "The physical and mental sufferings which this slow death involved are unimaginable" (J. Schneider).

Think of the utter horror the convicted criminal felt when he heard the sentence pronounced, "Crucify him!" The cross meant suffering, agony and death. Yet Jesus calls us to "take up our cross." What is He saying!

1) *The man who took up his cross was going to the place of death.* He was saying "Good-bye" to this world. He would never again see his loved ones here. His old plans and pursuits were finished. He was reaching the end of his life. What a frightful thing it must have been to take up the cross! Yet in Jesus, this is the first step to freedom: "For whoever wants to save his life will lose it, but whoever loses his life for Me will find it" (Matt. 16:25).

Have *we* lost our lives for Him? "We know the Lord Jesus became fruitful, not by bearing the Cross merely, but by dying on it" (Hudson Taylor).

It's so easy to sound religious and holy. It's so easy to use pious terms. But how many of us have really died? How many of us can truthfully say, "Lord, not my will but Your will be done" — *whatever God's will may be?*

Losing your life is traumatic. We are survivors by instinct and nature. We feel secure when we have control — when we are holding fast to the pride of our lives. Our careers, our goals, our desires — they cry out to us to be fulfilled. Following Jesus means death to *our* lives. Following Jesus means the end of *our* dreams. Following Jesus means the end of *self*-rule. It is all or nothing. Gaining the Son means giving up the sin. The choices are simple and clear. "No one who puts his hand to the plow and looks back is fit for the kingdom of God" (Luke 9:62).

2) *The crucified man was done with sin because dead men sin no more.* Lusts and fleshly passions became a thing of the past. The crucified thief could steal no more; the crucified murderer could no longer kill. Carnal cravings could never again be fulfilled. Sinful pleasures were over forever. The "flesh" had been nailed to a tree. And this is what happened to us!

"For we know that our old self was crucified with Him so that the body of sin might be done away with, that we should no longer be slaves to sin — *because anyone who has died has been freed from sin*" (Rom. 6:6-7).

"Therefore since Christ suffered in His body, arm yourselves also with the same attitude, because *he who has suffered in his body is done with sin.* As a result, he does not live the rest of his earthly life for evil human desires, but rather for the will of God" (1 Pet. 4:1-2). Those are powerful words!

Let's stop and give thought to our ways. Do we realize that we no longer have the right to sin? Do we understand that it's all over for the flesh? Has it finally settled in that, as far as the old man is concerned, we cannot do what we want (Gal. 5:17)?

"*Put to death,* therefore, whatever belongs to your earthly nature: sexual immorality, impurity, lust, evil desires and greed, which is idolatry. . . . You used to walk in these ways, in the life you once lived" (Col. 3:5,7). But now you have died to it all! The man or woman who willfully walks in sin has not taken up the cross.

Are we still watching movies with profanity, nudity and glorified violence? In Jesus we are dead to all that! Are we still lying, cheating, or walking in bitterness, pride or greed? That nature was nailed to a tree! "But now you must rid yourselves of all such things as these: anger, rage, malice, slander, and filthy language from your lips" (Col. 3:8). The Scripture says *must.*

What if we refuse to repent? "Because of such things God's wrath comes on those who are disobedient" (Eph. 5:6). This is no time to play games! He will help those who struggle, who really hate sin, who in brokenness call out for grace. But we should tremble for those who, in stubborn pride, try to justify their carnal lives and, in the name of "balance," seek to legitimize their worldly lusts.

3) *Taking up the cross is the ultimate form of self-denial.* In the deepest possible sense, the crucified man was no longer his own. Do you recall the Lord's words to Peter? "I tell you the truth, when you were younger you dressed yourself and went where you wanted; but when you are old you will stretch out your hands, and *someone else will dress you and lead you where you do not want to go* " (John 21:18). He was speaking of death on a cross!

Your hands are stretched out, you are nailed to the beam, you hang from the air — there is nothing you can do! You'd rather stop breathing — but you can't even die! Your life is no longer your own. "If anyone would come after Me, he must *deny himself* and *take up his cross daily* and follow Me" (Luke 9:23).

What does it mean to deny ourselves? It has nothing to do with self-torture — with whipping ourselves, wearing sackcloth and ashes, and moping about in despair. "Such regulations indeed have an appearance of wisdom, with their self-imposed worship, their false humility, and their harsh treatment of the body, but they lack any value in restraining sensual indulgence" (Col. 2:23). They bear no spiritual fruit.

Denying the self means saying "No" to *our* desires, whatever the consequence or cost. "An easy, non-self denying life will never be one of power. Fruit-bearing involves cross-bearing. Are you willing to abide in Him and thus bear much fruit?" (Hudson Taylor)

Look for a moment at the needs of the world. There are more than 900 million Muslims across the globe today. How many workers are sharing the gospel with them? More than 150 thousand human beings for whom Jesus gave His life die every day. How many of them knew the Lord? Doesn't He want to reach them? Isn't He calling laborers forth? Then why do so few of us hear God's call to missions? Because we live so far from His voice!

The majority of us here in the U.S.A. are the by-products of a luxury society. We often work only five days out of seven. (Compared to some other countries, this is practically a vacation!) We have much leisure time on our hands and most of us experience no hunger or starvation. Yet with so much time to pray, and with bodies that are often overfed, so few of us hear God's call to sacrificial prayer and fasting. Why? Because we are more sensitive to our flesh than to the Spirit!

The cults are everywhere at work, making gains both here and abroad. Some come aggressively and knock on our doors.

Others stand on street corners and chant. Some work outdoors in the rain and the cold. They sacrifice and serve and give. And none of them even have life! We have the truth. We have the light. We know the joy of the Lord. Then why do so few of us hear God's call to rise up and boldly share? Because we are too busy doing our own thing!

Oh, it's not because we don't care. It's not because we're totally unconcerned. But as A. W. Tozer has stated so clearly: It's not that people don't want God — it's that people "found something they wanted more than God!" We are determined to have what we want most. "The rich young ruler made his decision on the basis of what he wanted most in life (Tozer)". He wanted Jesus, but he wanted his wealth more. He went away sad because in his case, as a lover of money, he couldn't have both.

Now, let's look at our lives and look back to the cross. What is it we want the most?

4) *The cross is the only way to the resurrection.* Nobody wants to die. Nobody likes to suffer. But "unless a kernel of wheat falls to the ground and dies, it remains only a single seed. But if it dies, it produces many seeds" (John 12:24). There is no other way.

How we love the resurrection glory! We love the Spirit's power and His gifts. But first we have to die. First we have to be buried. *God can only raise up dead men.*

Look at the Apostle Paul. He was literally a holy terror. He prayed without ceasing, preached without cowering, raised the dead, and rattled the devil. But what was the key to his life? He died and no longer lived! Now Messiah was living in him.

"I worked harder than all of [the apostles] — *yet not I,* but the grace of God that was with me . . . [As for me] I die every day" (1 Cor. 15:10,31).

"I labor, struggling *with all His energy,* which so powerfully works in me" (Col. 1:29).

"In our hearts we felt the sentence of death. But this happened that *we might not rely on ourselves* but on God, who raises the dead" (2 Cor. 1:9).

God has called us to an impossible task — to make disciples of the nations, to heal the sick, to destroy the works of darkness, to prepare the way for Jesus' return. In our strength it can never be done. But that is the glorious answer: Quit striving! Give up and die. Come to the end of all self-dependence. Become like Jesus in His death (Phil. 3:10). And then share in His resurrection life.

John Wesley sent Francis Asbury to America in 1771. But the odds were plainly against him. He was a school dropout, he was not a great speaker (the general populace thought his illiterate black servant was more eloquent), and he was plagued by ill health (at times "he forced himself to stay in the saddle, even when covered by blisters"). Yet he found a strength greater than his own.

He "rose every morning at four o'clock, taught himself Latin, Greek, and Hebrew, and made it his rule to read 100 pages of good literature *daily . . . ; he preached well over 16,000 sermons, ordained more than 4,000 preachers, traveled on horseback or (when he was too old for that) in carriage 270,000 miles [remember, there were no highways in his day], and wore out six faithful horses!" (Christian History)*

When he arrived here in 1771, "there were only 600 *American* Methodists. But when he died 45 years later, there were 214,235 American Methodists. The number soared from 1 in 5,000 to 1 in 40 of the total population" (Charles Ludwig). All this from a man expected to fail!

Can you fathom the power of God? The worker is only a vessel. There is no mighty Asbury or Paul. Only One is worthy of praise. And He simply wants *us* to die. For the way to God's life is by death, and the end of our strength means the beginning of His.

Let's face the cross boldly and die. Let's kill fleshly lusts for all time. Let's crush all self-will and obey. Let's be crucified, buried and raised — by the power of the Spirit of God.

"Now to Him who is able to do immeasurably more than all we ask or imagine, *according to His power that is at work within us,* to Him be glory in the church and in Christ Jesus throughout all generations, for ever and ever! Amen" (Eph. 3:20-21).

Chapter Three

What It Means
To Be Born Again

There is no experience in life like childbirth. After nine months of waiting, and often hours of painful labor, a new human being is born. A tiny person emerges from its mother's womb. The baby is breathing and moving and crying. The proud parents are thrilled and relieved. What a moment, what a joy, what a sight!

But wait one second. We left someone out. The parents' experience is relatively minor. Sure the new dad is elated. Sure the tired mom is overwhelmed. But what do you think it felt like to be the baby? How did it feel to be born? Now *that* is the real adventure! From the womb to the world — there is nothing like being born!

Jesus said, "You must be born again" (John 3:7). This sounds like upheaval!

Think of starting a whole new life. That is being born once again.

Think of having a clean new slate. That is being born once again.

Think of passing into a whole other realm. That is being born once again.

Think of becoming a child of God. That is being born once again.

"For you were once darkness, but now you are light in the Lord. Live as children of light" (Eph. 5:8).

"As for you, you were dead in your transgressions and sins, in which you used to live . . . But because of His great love for us, God, who is rich in mercy, made us alive with Christ even when we were dead in transgressions — it is by grace you have been saved" (Eph. 2:1-2,4-5).

"For He has rescued us from the dominion of darkness and brought us into the kingdom of the Son He loves" (Col. 1:13). Thank God for new birth in Him!

John Newton was a notorious sinner. Although he was raised in the Lord by his godly mother, she died when he was seven. By the age of 11 he was working at sea with his father. He soon suffered miserable treatment and deprivation; he became hardened and blasphemous to the very core of his being. As he grew up and took over his own ships, his reputation as a profane and merciless slave trader was known far and wide.

It was John Newton who wrote the words, "Amazing grace how sweet the sound, that saved a wretch like me; I once was lost but now am found, was blind but now I see." John Newton was born again! And this is what has happened to us, if Jesus is truly our Lord.

We have received a new nature and bear the fresh image of God. There is a "new self, created to be like [Him] in true righteousness and holiness" (Eph. 4:24). We have been born from above. "The old has gone, the new has come" — we are brand new creations in Him (2 Cor. 5:17). Some of us were wicked, immoral, hateful and corrupt. Now we are washed, sanctified and justified, "in the name of the Lord Jesus and by the Spirit of our God" (1 Cor. 6:9-11). Something revolutionary has happened. We have truly been born again!

Is this what we are preaching to the people? Are we making the new birth clear? Do we tell them that everything will change? Do they fully understand that the second birth is no less dramatic than the first birth? Do they realize that they are about to enter a new family, and that they are passing from death into life?

Of course, they don't have to *feel* anything happening; they don't have to cry or to shout. But if their lives are not inwardly affected, if they don't soon experience a fundamental change of character, if they continue to live as they did, it is doubtful that they were born again! It is not always a matter of poor follow-up. As a pastor once said, "The reason why some people 'backslide' is because they never 'frontslid.' "

Have you ever wondered about evangelistic statistics? — 300 saved at the rally last night; 484 decisions through the outreach campaign; 1500 new births during the "revival" meetings last month. But what happened to all the people? Where are all the numbers today? Most of them just faded into the woodwork. They prayed a small prayer and went home. Were they ever truly *saved* from their sins? Can we say they were born from above?

Our gospel message has been doubly defective. We have injured our hearers in two ways: We have failed to tell them the old life must end; and we have failed to show them new life in Him.

Think of what would happen to someone who joined the Hare Krishna's. Do you think he would undergo change? If he once had aspirations to be an actor, he could forget about that for good. There are not many leading roles for men with shaved heads, beads and gowns! What if he had wanted to play professional football? Do you think they would let him on the field?

What would happen to someone who seriously converted to Islam? He'd be up at the crack of dawn for the first of his *five* times of daily prayer. He would fast until sundown during the whole Muslim month of Ramadan — that means no eating *or* drinking every day until evening. He would give 2.5 percent of his net worth — excluding obligations and family expenses — to the faith. The customs go on and on.

What about Ultra-Orthodox Judaism? What demands would be made on the Jew who fully returned to tradition? He would be told how to dress, how to pray, what to eat (sorry, but no more lobsters, shrimp, pepperoni pizza, or steak with baked potatoes and butter!). He would learn how to study, how to live — down to the smallest, most minute details of life. It would affect where he resided (within walking distance of the synagogue) and even how he washed his hands before meals.

And this is what really hurts: all these cults or religions cannot transform the inner nature of their adherents or bring them into a personal relationship with God. Legalism and external regulations do not produce eternal life. Yet people are flocking into these groups by the thousands. They will pay any price and make any sacrifice to live out their new found faith.

Yet we apologetically try to present the gospel to our hearers as if they would be doing Jesus a favor by receiving Him into their hearts. We tell them, "It's okay. Don't worry about change. You really don't have to forsake anything. Just ask Jesus to come in!" But *He* is the Lord of all, and He says, "You come to Me!" *He* is the pearl of great price. *We* are indebted to *Him.*

"The trouble is the whole 'Accept Christ' attitude is likely to be wrong. It shows Christ applying to us rather than us to Him. It makes Him stand hat-in-hand awaiting our verdict on Him, instead of our kneeling with troubled hearts awaiting His verdict on us. It may even permit us to accept Christ by an impulse of mind or emotions, painlessly, at no loss to our ego and no inconvenience to our usual way of life" (A. W. Tozer). But Jesus and the old life don't mix. We are called to press upward to Him.

How would a young man feel after he proposed to the woman he loved if she looked at him and said: "Yes, I'll marry you. But do I have to give up my other boyfriends? Will you want me back home every night? Can I still sleep around and have fun?" What would his reaction be? He would be hurt and disappointed. He would be deeply shattered and shocked. He expected her unswerving loyalty. He wanted a true mate for life.

What about Jesus our heavenly Bridegroom? Does He deserve less than that? Will He accept sinners if they do not pledge Him their loyalty? Yet we are afraid to tell the unregenerate that they must give up their "other lovers" if they want to be joined to Him. We don't want to turn them off! What a pitiful mentality.

In the late 1950's Mickey Cohen, a notorious gangster, attended an evangelistic meeting in Beverly Hills. Although he expressed some interest in the message, he "made no commitment until some time later when another friend urged him, using Revelation 3:20 as a warrant, to invite Jesus Christ into his life. This he professed to do, but his life subsequently gave no evidence of repentance, 'that mighty change of mind, heart and life' [Trench]. He rebuked [the] friend, telling him: 'You did not tell me that I would have to give up my work,' meaning his rackets; 'You did not tell me that I would have to give up my friends,' meaning his gangster associates. He had heard that so-and-so was a Christian football player, so-and-so a Christian cowboy, so-and-so a Christian actress, so-and-so a Christian senator, and he really thought that he could be a Christian gangster. Alas, there was not evidence of repentance. Many have sadly forgotten that the only evidence of the new birth is the new life. The real problem is that some evangelists, like some converts, have failed to realize that the fault lies in the defective message" (J. Edwin Orr).

Why are we playing games? Why are we trying to make God seem just in the eyes of man when it is man who needs to be just in the eyes of God? Why are we trying to make the gospel seem palatable to blind and lost sinners? Why aren't we boldly challenging them to throw off their sinful lifestyles, to forsake their futile ways, and to *run* to the light and be saved? Why aren't we telling them: "Your way is death. Your way means hell. Choose life and repent of your sin." Why aren't we letting them know that Jesus is THE answer — that forsaking everything is *nothing* in the light of gaining Him?

Stop and think for a moment. God's holy Son died for the world. The spotless One suffered a criminal's death. He bore all our sins on the tree. The Righteous Lamb died for foul sinners. The Prince paid the price for our crimes. We sinned. He died. We were guilty. He was punished. We deserved death. He gave us His life. We rejected Him. He accepted us. *What an incredible message.* It seems far too good to be true.

But that is only the beginning. There is more that we have to proclaim. The same Spirit who raised Jesus from the dead comes to abide in us. We receive eternal life. Our names are written in heaven. We are ransomed, restored and renewed. We enjoy intimacy with almighty God, and Jesus calls us His friends.

So why are we belittling the Lord as if He were part of a cheap bargain special? Why are we appealing to the lost to squeeze Jesus in and give Him a chance? Why aren't we being direct? Let's wake up and be honest. Let's preach Jesus for all that He's worth. Let's boldly announce the new birth and call sinners to be born again. And let's radically live out the message.

God's new life is bursting within.

Chapter Four

Were You Ever Lost?

Jesus said, "It is not the healthy who need a doctor, but the sick" (Matt. 9:13). Even God cannot heal a well person! Only sick people can be healed. In the same way, only sinners can be forgiven, and only the lost can be saved. Jesus died for the lost alone.

On one occasion, George Whitefield was preaching to a small gathering of British nobility. Lord Chesterfield, who was always fascinated by Whitefield's illustrations, was listening intently. John Pollock tells the story:

"Whitefield had said that a man without Christ resembled a blind [old] beggar with a stick, using his little dog as guide. They are walking on a grassy downland slope not knowing they are at the top of a cliff. The string breaks and the dog wanders off. The beggar desperately puts both hands on the stick and pokes his way forward as best he can. He draws nearer, nearer the cliff. He pokes the stick out once again and its point goes over the edge and the unexpected motion makes him drop it. (Whitefield's hearers were now taut with excitement.) The chasm is too high for an echo so the beggar thinks the stick has fallen into a soft shallow ditch. He leans over to feel. He loses his balance, his foot slips . . .

" 'He's gone!' Lord Chesterfield yelled," leaping to his feet.

That is the description of the whole human race — "They're gone!" And the hour is late.

Most of us are still waiting to hear the full gospel. Our modern version leaves much to be desired. We love to preach on heaven, but hardly say a word about hell. We make long appeals for salvation, but damnation sounds like a dirty word. We talk about the cross and the blood, but Jesus seems to hang there for nothing. Why in the world did He die?

The cross makes sense only if mankind is hopelessly lost, only if no one can be just in God's eyes, only if all of us have fallen infinitely short, only if we truly deserve the sentence of death, only if He would be perfectly fair in condemning us forever, only if we can do nothing to save ourselves. Only then does the cross makes sense. Otherwise it is the ultimate divine waste — Jesus suffered and bled for no reason. "I do not set aside the grace of God, for if righteousness could be gained through the law, Christ died for nothing" (Gal. 2:21).

Our gospel has failed to attack one of the basic plagues of our race: self-righteousness. Is there any sin God hates more than this? Self-righteousness is idolatry. Self-righteousness makes man into god and sets its own standards. Self-righteousness brings a foul curse. "This is what the Lord says: 'Cursed is the one who trusts in man, who depends on flesh for his strength and whose heart turns away from the Lord" (Jer. 17:5). "Go and learn what that means: 'I desire mercy, not sacrifice.' For I have not come to call the righteous, but sinners" (Matt. 9:13). God can not help the self-righteous man.

Why do we have so many proud, self-sufficient believers in our congregations? Why is there so little brokenness in our midst? Why do some of our preachers seem to show off and strut? Why are we so quick to praise man? It is because we have not seen the depth of our sin. We have not grasped our lost state without God. We have not comprehended our natural condition — not diseased, but decomposing; not critical, but a corpse! The unsaved human being is dead; he cannot resurrect himself.

We must approach the unsaved with this reality. "Take the bandage off their eyes which Satan has bound round them; knock and hammer and burn in, with the fire of the Holy Ghost, your words into their poor hardened, darkened hearts, until they begin to realise that they are IN DANGER; that there is something amiss. Go after them" (Catherine Booth). They are *perishing* without the Lord.

When Peter preached on the Day of Pentecost, the people "were cut to the heart and said to Peter and the other apostles, 'Brothers, what shall we do?' " (Acts 2:37). Why were they so convicted? What was it that challenged them so? "Let all Israel be assured of this: God has made this Jesus, whom you crucified, both Lord and Christ" (Acts 2:36). What a horror, what a shock, what a jolt. We crucified our Messiah! We nailed the hope of Israel to a tree! And now He sits enthroned as Lord. Brothers, help us! What shall we do?

When people see the greatness of their sin, when they recognize that they can do nothing to remove their guilt, when they understand that judgment is near, they will "flee from the coming wrath" (Matt. 3:7), crying "What must I do to be saved?" (Acts 16:30). Suddenly God's grace seems so big!

"Was ever the remembrance of your sins grievous to you? Was the burden of your sins intolerable to your thoughts? Did you ever see that God's wrath might justly fall upon you, on account of your actual transgressions against God? Were you ever in all your life sorry for your sins? Could you ever say, My sins are gone over my head as a burden too heavy for me to bear? Did you ever experience any such thing as this? If not, for Jesus Christ's sake, do not call yourselves Christians; you may speak peace to your hearts, but there is no peace. May the Lord awaken you, may the Lord convert you, may the Lord give you peace . . . before you go home!" (George Whitefield)

Consider the words of the Lord:

"Once the owner of the house gets up and closes the door, you will stand outside knocking and pleading, 'Sir, open the door for us.' But he will answer, 'I don't know you or where you come from . . . Away from Me, all you evildoers!' There will be weeping there, and gnashing of teeth, when you see Abraham, Isaac and Jacob and all the prophets of God, *but you yourselves thrown out"*(Luke 13:25,27-28).

What an overwhelming thought. Some people will be *thrown out*! There will be *weeping and gnashing of teeth* — utter darkness and no relief. And to think of the bitter indictment: We haven't told people the truth!

"Here is the sinner in rebellion. God comes with pardon in one hand and a sword in the other, and tells the sinner to repent and receive pardon, or refuse and perish" (Charles Finney). Is this the gospel we preach?

Listen to Finney again:

"It is of great importance that the sinner should be made to *feel his guilt*, and not left to the impression that he is *unfortunate*. I think this is a very prevalent fault, particularly in books on the subject. They are calculated to make the sinner think more of his sorrows than of his sin, and feel that his state is rather *unfortunate* than criminal.

"Make the sinner see that all pleas in excuse for not submitting to God, are acts of rebellion against Him. Tear away the last LIE which he grasps in his hand, and make him feel that he is absolutely condemned before God." This is the gospel of grace.

"I preached from George Whitefield's pulpit, the wall . . . Many, I am persuaded, found themselves stripped, wounded, and half-dead; *and are therefore ready for the oil and wine"* (Charles Wesley). The patients were prepared for surgery. It was time for mercy to come forth.

* * *

If we truly realized that we were once lost without hope, we would be grateful to God beyond words — for he who is forgiven much, loves much (Luke 7:40-50). Could anyone be more precious to us than Jesus, who took the Father's wrath *for us?*

At the age of fifteen, newly converted Hudson Taylor had a special time of communion with the Lord. "Well do I remember that occasion. How in the gladness of my heart I poured out my soul before God; and again and again confessing my grateful love to Him who had done everything for me — who had saved me when I had given up all hope and even desire for salvation — I besought Him to give me some work to do for Him, as an outlet for love and gratitude; some self-denying service, no matter what it might be, however trying or however trivial; something with which He would be pleased, and that I might do for Him who had done so much for me." He has done so much for us!

John "Praying" Hyde, missionary to India, was raised in the faith and never fell into the ways of the world. Yet he still realized how great his own sin was and how deeply he needed God's grace. Jesus was Hyde's blessed Savior, and salvation was priceless in his eyes. "Years ago I felt that I wanted to give something to Jesus Christ who loved me so, and I gave myself to Him absolutely, and promised Him that no one should come into my life and share my affection for Him. I told the Lord that I would not marry, but be His altogether." Married or single, should we love any less?

If we truly realized that we were once lost without hope, we would stop at nothing and call no sacrifice too great in order to reach other lost sinners with the Good News. It is for this reason that countless missionaries have given up their lives, endured hardship and hunger, and suffered persecution and loss. After all, in light of so great a salvation, what else could they do? "When he found his own soul needed Jesus Christ, it became a passion with him to take Jesus Christ to every soul" (said of Jonathan Goforth, who gave himself to win the lost in China and Manchuria).

William C. Burns was born again in Scotland in 1832, and immediately he knew his great debt. "In the same instant almost I felt that I must leave my present occupation, and devote myself to Jesus in the ministry of that glorious gospel by which I had been saved." Then, in 1847, at the age of thirty-one, after nine glorious years of revival preaching in and around Scotland, the door to the mission field finally opened. When asked how soon he could begin his work in China, he replied, "Tomorrow!" Years later, when he was convinced that he needed more laborers to join him in the China work, Burns donated his *whole year's salary* to his own missions board, telling them to send workers.

Consider also the experience of John G. Lake:
"When on the African mission fields, my wife, seven children, and I sat down an hundred times when we did not have a thing but corn meal mush, and sometimes did not have salt to put on it, yet I preached three or four times a day, and

ministered to the sick continuously. My heart is hungry for it now. I would say, 'Goodbye to your pumpkin pie and everything else,' and go back to mush, if I could have the same victory for Jesus Christ."

Once, when Lake was in Los Angeles, one of his missionaries wrote him from the heart of Basutoland. "Mr. Lake," he said, "the soles are worn out of my shoes, and my feet are bleeding, my shins are cut, and my body is sore." But Lake gave him no sympathy. "Brother, your shoes are worn-out and your feet are bleeding for the Lord Jesus Christ. Men's feet have bled and their body is sore in the service of the devil many a time, and surely we can go just as far and a little farther for the Son of God and eternal life."

And what happened to a passionate and broken Evan Roberts when, as he says, "the salvation of the human soul was impressed upon me"? "I felt ablaze with a desire to go through the length and breadth of Wales to tell of the Savior; and *had it been possible, I was willing to pay God for doing so.*"

This is how Paul shook his world:

"Though I am free and belong to no man, I make myself a slave to everyone, to win as many as possible. . . . I have become all things to all men so that by all possible means I might save some" (1 Cor. 9:19,22).

What about us? Do we owe any less?

Chapter Five

Our Gospel Has No Teeth!

Every year, more than ten thousand believers are being martyred. That's right. *More than 10,000 people* who proclaim Jesus as Lord are being put to death every year. How can this possibly be? Even if we say that this figure is too high (some experts claim that it's far too low!), even if it includes believers killed through indiscriminate terrorist attacks, as well as people who were murdered more for political reasons than spiritual reasons, even if there are only *one thousand* believers being martyred a year, this figure is still astounding to the American Christian mind.

Here in America, if one believer would be martyred, it would produce an outrage from coast to coast. It would shake up the people of God. It would make the headlines of every newspaper in the country. It would be a national event. We'd probably even make a movie about it!

Then what's the difference between America and Iran (where Muslims who convert can be killed on the spot), or between our country and Albania (where believers have been sealed in barrels and thrown out to sea)? Why is there virtually no persecution here? It is true that we are different than the Marxist and Islamic nations. Religious liberty for us is a constitutional right. We can evangelize and preach to our heart's content. And we have some godly people in our government. But is the United States a "Christian" nation? Hardly!

We have the highest level of teenage drug abuse in any industrialized nation, as well as the highest divorce rate. We are by far the world's largest manufacturer of beer and the third greatest consumer of alcohol per capita. "Christian" America has some of the world's most liberal abortion laws — we have *legally* murdered 25 million little ones since 1973, now killing 42 babies for every 100 live births. Prayer in our schools is against the law. Our children's textbooks honor Buddha and Mohammed, while many cynical, sarcastic professors provide our "higher education." The liberal media gives our people the news, and now our grocery stores peddle smut. Magazines that would have been hard to come by a few decades ago because of their sexual content are now placed on check-out counters for our children to see! *We are not a "Christian" nation!*

We have annual parades celebrating homosexual and lesbian behavior, and not even AIDS has slowed us down. In fact, when one congressman was recently exposed by his male prostitute companion, Congress was hesitant to try to remove him. Why? Because too many other senators were guilty of similar perversions! All of this is occuring among the elected officials governing our land — this "one nation under God."

Oh yes, thank God for America! Our country is one of the greatest countries that has ever existed, and we have so much to give. But remember, it is not so much Communism or Islam that stands against the gospel — it is the world. *And America is of the world.*

Why is it then that God's people suffer virtually no persecution here? *Because our gospel has no teeth!* It hardly exposes sin in the Body, let alone in the world. How are we shining the light? How are we confronting the world with the righteousness of God? How are we bringing a shaking to our society? Why do we hardly make anyone uncomfortable anymore?

The fact is, when we do poke the devil in the eye by protesting the murder of innocent babies, or by exposing the evils of pornography, the enemy rages and roars. We have dared to invade his guarded territory, and he doesn't like it one bit. But this is the exception, not the rule. The devil is still sitting safe and secure. He sees how ineffectual most of our words and actions are. And he sees how almost all of our ministry endeavors are designed to build up our own lives, not touch the world. *Are we merely fattening ourselves for slaughter?*

As American believers we have corporately spent hundreds of millions of dollars on our own edification while foreign workers could have evangelized hundreds of millions of their own unreached countrymen with the financial crumbs that fall from our tables. And to add insult to injury, despite all our efforts, our ministry to ourselves has left us inactive, passive and pathetically comfortable in a fallen, dying society. Is it any wonder that Satan is not afraid of our big talk? It hasn't shaken the Church. How can it shake the world?

The last few decades have seen a deluge of radio and television ministries. But according to every criterion of decency and morality, our national standard is down. What good has all our preaching done?

Lots of young people want "ministries." They are looking for opportunities to share the Scriptures. Well, there are plenty of street corners throughout our cities in need of young preachers with a message! God knows — we don't need more ministers serving our connoisseur congregations the latest in gourmet

Word! *We need to get out where the action is.* Then we'll see some results. Then the sparks will fly.

Take an example from the secular world. In 1989 when the United States government began working with Columbia to apprehend and extradite Columbia's big drug dealers, the repercussions were intense. The drug lords responded with wholesale violence — blowing up planes, murdering newspaper reporters, kidnapping innocent civilians, and bombing police headquarters. Why? Because they were being brought to account; their lifestyle was being threatened.

It is the same with the gospel. When we tell people that they are sinners, that there is a consequence to their actions, that one day they will be judged for their deeds, that without doubt a guilty verdict will come, people get enraged! But when all we say is "Only believe!" — no repentance, no commitment, no change of life required — why should there be any offense? How are we holding anyone accountable? How are we convicting them of their sin? We simply are not preaching the whole counsel of God. If we were (with so much media exposure), the American people would be trembling in their boots!

What if Paul and Peter were alive today, ministering in the United States? Wouldn't they be persecuted? Of course they would! Why? Because they would be a threat to the devil's operation. They would be making trouble for the powers of darkness. And they would be disturbing the ungodly who are living in sin.

Look at the Book of Acts. The apostles were beaten and stoned by idolaters and imprisoned by hypocritical religious authorities. Why? Because their message was a menace to the kingdom of darkness. It had an adverse effect on business!

Persecution arises when the gospel is a threat to a degenerate, perverted society and a cold, formalistic religious leadership. *Good business for the kingdom of God means bad business for the devil.* Of this we can rest assured: if we were making real inroads into Satan's empire, we would be feeling his heat. Instead we have become one with the world and one with the religious establishment. That's why we receive virtually no persecution from either.

Paul's message so affected the people of Ephesus that local idol sales dropped sharply. It led to a huge riot in the city because the silversmiths and craftsmen were afraid they would go bankrupt (Acts 19). But today in our great nation, we have the strangest of occurrences: "idol sales" and Bible sales are *both* on the increase. Although lots of people are getting "saved," there doesn't seem to be much less sinning! Our lives are so intertwined with this corrupt world that we no longer can bring a holy standard to it.

When the prophetic priest Girolamo Savonarola preached in Florence five hundred years ago, his message sent shock-waves through the whole city. "His sermons 'caused such terror and alarm, such sobbing and tears that people passed through the streets without speaking, more dead than alive' as he prophesied coming judgment on the church and the country" (Winkie Pratney, quoting Harold Fischer). *And his only weapon was words.*

"But as for me, I am filled with power, with the Spirit of the Lord, and with justice and might, to declare to Jacob his transgression, to Israel his sin" (Mic. 3:8). It was not long before Savonarola was imprisoned, tortured and executed — but not until Italy was confronted with the truth. May God give us a whole generation of fire-tongued, brokenhearted, holy men and women of the Spirit, to shatter this world's security by the power of the Word. Oh, for the sharp, piercing sword of truth!

When Stephen accused the religious leaders of his day of being stiff-necked and hardhearted, "they were furious and gnashed their teeth" (Acts 7:54). But today we are making no one mad. Our messages put people to sleep rather than make them weep; they are calculated to win men's praise, not to provoke their rage. Who are we confronting today? We have made our peace with the religious system.

We really are not much different than the "dead" church. We go to service on Sunday mornings, attend a mid-week Bible study or prayer meeting, *and leave our religion inside the sanctuary doors* (if we're serious enough to bring it home with us, we keep it locked in our houses!). Who in the world would want to persecute us? We are too harmless and mild.

Listen to the fiery words uttered in England by Catherine Booth over one-hundred years ago: "Opposition! It is a bad sign for the Christianity of this day that it provokes so little opposition. If there were no other evidence of it being wrong, I should know from that. When the Church and the world can jog along together comfortably, you may be sure there is something wrong. The world has not altered. Its spirit is exactly the same as it ever was, and if Christians were equally faithful and devoted to the Lord, and separated from the world, living so that their lives were a reproof to all ungodliness, the world would hate them as much as it ever did. It is the *Church* that has altered, *not* the world." How can we argue with this?

The Word is perfectly clear:
"*Everyone* who wants to live a godly life in Christ Jesus will be persecuted" (2 Tim. 3:12).
"If the world hates you, keep in mind that it hated Me first. If you belonged to the world, it would love you as its own. As it is, you do not belong to the world, but I have chosen you out of the world. That is why the world hates you. Remember the

words I spoke to you: 'No servant is greater than his master.' If they persecuted Me, they will persecute you also" (John 15:18-20).

There is no getting away from the plain sense of these verses: if we were living godly lives in the full sense of the biblical word, *we would be persecuted.* If we did not belong to the world, just as Jesus did not belong to the world, *we would be hated as He was hated.*

The people of the world today are still rejecting the Son of God.

Why aren't they rejecting us?

Chapter Six

In The World
And Of It

When Paul instructed the Corinthians not to "associate with anyone who *calls himself a brother* but is sexually immoral or greedy, an idolater or a slanderer, a drunkard or a swindler," he was careful to point out that he was *not* talking about the unsaved, but rather about those who claimed to be believers but were not living the life. Otherwise, he said, "you would have to leave the world" (1 Cor. 5:9-11). Nowadays things are different: to follow Paul's instructions, we would practically have to leave the Church!

In times past, the Church went into the world and converted the lost to the Lord. Today, the world has entered the Church and perverted the law of the Lord. Two thousand years ago, the ancient world was amazed by the disciples' courage. Today the modern world is amused by our carnality. Once we effectively evangelized the lost. Today we entertain them. We have more of a soap opera gospel than a sold out gospel.

And here is the tragedy of it all: we have adjusted our standards to the constantly declining standards of our society for so long that we do not even realize how far we have fallen.

Take the example of modest dress. At the end of the last century, if people went to the beach, they were practically covered from head to toe. Little by little, more skin was revealed until today almost anything goes.

So what do beach-loving believers do now? They go to the same "skin-infested" waters surrounded by half-naked bodies (actually, half-naked wouldn't be so bad!), but they wear "modest" bathing suits (some even try to justify "modest" bikinis). Modest!? Compared to what? To a modern day version of a couple of fig leaves? How dare we expose ourselves so freely! But, no! We're being conservative by the standards of the world. And what will we do if our country legalizes nude bathing? Will we *still* frequent these beaches? Will we try to develop a *modestly nude* look? God help us to see.

Recently, believers were outraged by the movie "The Last Temptation of Christ." Born again people throughout the land threatened to boycott movie theaters that showed this scandalous film. *But there was something much more scandalous than the movie itself* — it was that believers had clout at ungodly movie theaters! God's people could threaten corrupt Hollywood with a product boycott. What a horror!

We make such a habit of frequenting these theaters that the owners don't want to lose our business. *That* is the shame! There's not one recent Hollywood movie out of a hundred that God could ever smile at, and there isn't one new movie out of fifty that a blood-washed child of God should ever see. Why are we mingling with the world's pollutions?

When Marie Monson, a Norwegian missionary to China, was taken captive by Chinese pirates, she subsisted for two weeks on just three or four eggs a day rather than eat stolen food. The pirates would often come and urge her to eat more. But she would always reply, "No, I can't eat what you have looted." Yet we have had little or no problem freely giving our money to places that one week show blatant pornography and violence, and the next week some nice "family flick." Where is our sense of dignity and uprightness? Where is our abhorrence for sin?

Does it take a perverse attack on our Savior, like "The Last Temptation," to finally wake us up to the fact that, as sanctified sons and daughters of God, we have no business financing Hollywood? If there are godly producers and actors, let them come out of that mess, make a clean break, and take a stand for the Lord. If they want to be His witnesses *in the midst of Hollywood,* they had better walk in reverent, godly fear with an absolute no-compromise lifestyle. How many God-pleasing roles in non-offensive movies are there?

Listen to the standard of God:
"But among you there must not be even a hint of sexual immorality, or of any kind of impurity, or of greed, *because these are improper for God's holy people.* Nor should there be obscenity, foolish talk or coarse joking, which are out of place, but rather thanksgiving" (Eph. 5:3-4).
"Religion that God our Father accepts is this: to look after orphans and widows in their distress *and to keep oneself from being polluted by the world"* (James 1:27).
"Since we have these promises [of being sons and daughters of the Lord Almighty], let us purify ourselves from *everything* that contaminates body and spirit, *perfecting holiness* out of reverence for God" (2 Cor. 7:1).
What a glorious and challenging call!

Paul wrote to the Philippians to "do everything without complaining or arguing, so that you may become blameless and pure, children of God, without fault in a crooked and depraved generation, in which you shine like stars in the universe as you hold out the word of life" (Phil. 2:14-16). That must be our determined goal — to put no stumbling block before the world by our foolish actions, to shine forth and stand out because of our purity and holiness, and to clearly, boldly and uncompromisingly proclaim the living Word. But as long as we try to win the world by conforming to its ways, our only battle will be to survive!

It's time for us to repair our ways. We *must* reorder our lives. We must begin on our knees with open Bibles and open hearts. Before we can rebuke the sin that's in the land, we have to remove the sin that's in our lives. Before we can call for truth and justice, we have to passionately hate untruth and injustice. We must look carefully at ourselves in full light of the Word and ask God to open our hearts. We must not leave any stone unturned! It is better to face rigorous scrutiny *now*, than on that Day.

Maybe there are unacceptable areas of our lives that we never even thought to question. Clean fun, family time, fellowship and necessary relaxation are certainly *not* the problem. Contamination and compromise are. How much has our thinking been influenced by the ungodly? How deeply is our whole sense of values determined by this world's priorities? Has sinful peer pressure and the desire to be accepted caused a weakening in our stance before God? Just who are we living to please?

Maybe there are areas of blatant sin (they can only go unnoticed when, for months and months, we walk at a distance from God). Have you ever heard someone say, "Oh, the language in that movie didn't bother me that much. It used to offend me, but not any more." (Forget about X-rated and R-rated movies; PG-rated is bad enough!) "Sure, some of the sex scenes weren't exactly holy. But I'll tell you, I've seen a lot worse!" — as if the goal of our lives of faith was to see just how far we could sink into sin without actually drowning in it! Some people even think that being able to watch or read trash without being consciously polluted is a sign of maturity!

In fact it is a sure sign of deep hardening. The believer who finds himself in that state had better quickly and seriously repent. And what child of God in his right mind would even *want* the liberty to be exposed to such garbage? Forget the line about not being fanatical. We are in no danger of becoming fanatics! Actually, "the church has been subnormal for so long that when it finally becomes normal, it appears to be abnormal" (Leonard Ravenhill). God is asking for nothing extreme from us. He is just calling us back to the biblical norm. *We barely even know where to start.*

We have been like the proverbial frog being boiled alive in water. As the water temperature slowly rises, the frog's temperature rises right along with it. By the time he realizes what's happening, it's too late. Brothers and sisters, hear the warning: the water is beginning to boil and we still feel at home in the pot! Let's jump out while we still have life. Now is the time to make a decisive move. Now is the time to thoroughly clean house.

"Dear friends, I urge you as aliens and strangers in the world, to abstain from sinful desires, which war against your soul. Live such good lives among the pagans that, though they accuse you of doing wrong, they may see your good deeds and glorify God on the day He visits us" (1 Pet. 2:11-12). Our very lives can shine for the Lord.

Smith Wigglesworth shares with us:
"I remember one time stepping out of a railroad car to wash my hands. I had a season of prayer, and the Lord just filled me to overflowing with His love. I was going to a convention in

Ireland, and I could not get there fast enough. As I returned, I believe that the Spirit of the Lord was so heavily upon me that my face must have shone. (No man can tell himself when the Spirit transforms his very countenance.) There were two clerical men sitting together, and as I got into the carriage again, one of them cried out, 'You convict me of sin.' Within three minutes everyone in the car was crying to God for salvation. This thing has happened many times in my life. It is this ministration of the Spirit that Paul speaks of [2 Cor. 3], this filling of the Spirit that will make your life effective so that even the people in the stores where you trade will want to leave your presence because they are brought under conviction." This is the potential of the truly committed life.

All this begins as we come out of the world, and die to what once held us captive. It begins as we radically reevaluate our compromised lifestyles and become consecrated children of God.

We have little conception of just how far we have fallen.

Chapter Seven

Leaning On The Arm Of Flesh

Isaiah would be shocked. Ezekiel would be shaken. Jeremiah would be shattered. If these prophets were alive today, they would barely believe what their eyes would see. *There is an abomination in the household of God.*

Unsaved marketing experts write appeal letters for money-starved ministries . . .

Huge computer printers spew out mass produced "personal prophetic words" by the thousands . . .

Women in skin tight bodysuits advertise the latest in "Christian aerobics" . . .

TV preachers in costly apparel promise you riches if you send tithes to their ministry . . .

The blood-washed Church of the Son of God has gone Madison Avenue. Let the prophets weep and wail! The mighty have fallen — and fallen and fallen. Who would have thought we could have stooped so low?

The children of the Lord are hiring out the people of the world to help raise funds for the work of God. Sons of darkness are being consulted on how to merchandise the gospel of light.

The hand of God has become attached to an arm of flesh. How can this possibly be?

There was a talented young man in the fund raising industry. He had written many outstanding appeals for religious and secular clients alike. His prize winning letters hung framed on his office wall. He knew how to bring in the bucks. But he didn't know the Lord at all.

He had just finished writing an emergency plea for a prominent international ministry when he received word that his Christian grandmother was dying. He rushed to her side. But she had only one concern. She had to get her social security check mailed out *to that very ministry* before she died. She had just received their urgent appeal. They desperately needed her help. Could her grandson please send out the funds — before it was too late?

Little did she know that it was not her beloved "TV pastor" who wrote the letter. Little did she know that she was being moved by worldly psychological pressure and not the Spirit. And that young man, her own grandson, was to blame.

He was so shaken up when he saw the effects of his letter that he said, "Never again." He swore off the business for life. But the ministry that hired him just marched right on. How many other dying grandmothers did they plunder? How many poor widows sent in their last dollar? And how much of that money was paid out to the marketing company? How much actually went into the work of the Lord?

Five centuries ago in Germany there was a corrupt Catholic monk named Johann Tetzel. He popularized the perverse doctrine of indulgences: just give some money to the Church and all your sins will be forgiven. In fact, if you give enough, your loved ones will be freed from the fires of purgatory! "At the very instant that the money rattles at the bottom of the chest," Tetzel exclaimed, "the soul escapes from purgatory, and flies liberated to heaven." What a horrible doctrine! Yet the people bought it hook, line and sinker. It brought cart loads of money into the Church. And it also brought the judgment of God. It was not long before the Reformation shook Europe.

But there is a strangely familiar sound in the air today. It's almost as if there are Tetzels again in our midst! "If you give sacrificially to our ministry, you will be healed, your unsaved children will be born again, your marriage will be restored, and God will make you rich!" All this for your sizable gift — as long as you give to *their* work!

But where in the Word is any of this? Where does God ever say, "Plant a financial seed and reap your miracle — whatever your need might be"? When did Jesus ever say to a blind man, "Just contribute to My organization and I'll give you your sight"? And why do we have to give to *one particular* "super-anointed" work? Can't God bless us if we simply tithe to our home congregation and give offerings to the missionaries we send out? Did Paul ever say, "You'll be specially blessed if you contribute to *my* ministry — I have an exclusive arrangement with the Lord"?

Maybe these leaders who promise us almost anything if we will only give enough to their ministries are not intentionally trying to deceive us. But is it possible they have deceived themselves? Has the need to generate funds for their work driven them to resurrect Tetzel's mercenary ways? It is true — God pours out good things on those who give to Him in faith. It is true — when we are freed from covetousness and stinginess, a window of blessing is opened up to us. But once again, God's holy promises have been perverted for "the good of the

Church and the sake of the world." *Another reformation may be near.*

Ahaziah was an ungodly Israelite king who was badly injured in a fall. He sent messengers to inquire of a Philistine god to see if he would recover. But Elijah the prophet intercepted the king's messengers and gave Ahaziah a word of rebuke from the Lord:

"Is it because there is no God in Israel that you are going off to consult Baal-Zebub, the god of Ekron? Therefore this is what the Lord says: 'You will not leave the bed you are lying on. You will certainly die!' " (2 Kin. 1:1-4)

If King Ahaziah had been right with the Lord, he would not have needed to inquire of a pagan idol. God would have delivered him. The same holds true for us. When we are right with the Lord, He comes through for us every time.

So why are we consulting foreign gods? If we were walking in the center of God's will, wouldn't He meet our needs? The fact that some of us cannot lean on God alone is evidence that He is not backing us up. He is not coming through for us! If He was, why would we have to lean on the arm of flesh and go the way of the world? Wasn't this the constant battle of the Old Testament prophets — to keep Israel from trusting in the help of foreign armies and gods, to demand that Israel trust in the Lord alone?

What was the sin of king Asa of Judah? Early in his reign, Judah was attacked by the Cushites. Asa's army was hopelessly outnumbered. But he put his trust in the Lord alone and a great deliverance was wrought. As a result, Asa and the people "entered into a covenant to seek the Lord, the God of their fathers, with all their heart and all their soul. All who would not seek the Lord, the God of Israel, were to be put to death, whether small or great, man or woman" (2 Chr. 14, 15:12-13).

But in the thirty-sixth year of Asa's rule over Judah, Israel attacked him from the north. This time he called for the help of man, *taking the silver and gold out of the Temple of the Lord* to pay for the services of the Aramean army. God's treasures were used to hire out idol-worshiping, foreign troops to fight the battles of the Lord! Hanani the seer rebuked him:

"Because you relied on the king of Aram and not on the Lord your God, the army of the king of Aram has escaped from your hand. Were not the Cushites and Libyans a mighty army with great numbers of chariots and horsemen? Yet when you relied on the Lord, He delivered them into your hand. For the eyes of the Lord range throughout the earth to strengthen those whose hearts are fully committed to him. You have done a foolish thing, and from now on you will be at war" (2 Chr. 16:7-9).

The enraged king put Hanani in prison and "brutally oppressed some of the people" (2 Chr. 16:10). Then, in the thirty-ninth year of his reign, Asa was afflicted with a terrible disease in his feet. Although his disease was severe, even in his affliction he did not *seek the Lord,* but rather *inquired of the physicians* (he sought magical, pagan help from idolatrous physicians — that is the clear sense of the Hebrew in verse 12). All this from a king whose name originally meant "God has healed"!

But the story is not yet over. *There are many Asa-like ministries in our land.* In the beginning they walked by faith and trusted God — and He always came through for them in a big way. Many of them even put the word "faith" in their ministry slogan or name. But when pressures mounted, they turned to the flesh — as if the help of man was more certain than the help of God! Like Asa, they used the precious treasures of the house of the Lord — the sacrificial contributions of the people of God — to hire out fleshly support. Even in their great affliction, they did not fully seek the Lord, but put their trust instead in the enterprising arm of man. What a shame!

There are ministries today that resort to every kind of fleshly, high pressure, emotional tactic to stay afloat. Why? Because they are trying to perpetuate that which God has forsaken. They are desperately striving to prop up something that the Lord is not supporting. What began in the Spirit is now being carried out in the flesh. The heavenly aroma is gone. In fact, something stinks.

What kind of example are we setting with this kind of behavior? As Charles Stanley has said, we teach the people that God can supply all their needs and then tell them if they don't send in enough money, our ministries will fold. We exhort the people to believe that the battle belongs to the Lord and then tell them if they don't stand with us we'll lose the war. We preach prayer and petition, but practice persuasion and pleading. When will we learn our lesson?

"No king is saved by the size of his army; no warrior escapes by his great strength. A horse is a vain hope for deliverance; despite all its great strength it cannot save. [Today this might read: No ministry is saved by the size of its mailing list; no preacher escapes by his eloquence. A big bank account is a vain hope for deliverance; despite all its great assets it cannot save.] But the eyes of the Lord are on those who fear him, on those whose hope is in his unfailing love, *to deliver them from death* [that includes going off the air!] and *keep them alive in famine* [financial as well as physical!]" (Ps. 33:16-19). Yes, "some trust in chariots and some in horses, *but we trust in the name of the Lord our God*" (Ps. 20:7). Can this be our confession as well?

In 1865, Hudson Taylor established the China Inland Mission as a total work of faith. His prospective missionaries were not allowed to take offerings or make any direct appeals for money. They were not guaranteed a set salary, but were to depend entirely on God to meet their needs. Yet by 1934, almost 30 years after Taylor's death, there were 1368 workers on the field — and God was supplying for them! This was Taylor's conviction: *"Depend upon it. God's work done in God's way will never lack God's supplies."* This principle has never changed.

It was George Mueller's example that inspired Hudson Taylor. Mueller too had made a determination: "No more going to man instead of going to the Lord." If God is in the work, He can make it stand. If not, then let it fall! The Word is totally clear on this point: "Unless the Lord builds the house, its builders labor in vain. Unless the Lord watches over the city, the watchmen stand guard in vain" (Ps. 127:1). As someone said recently, "God does not appreciate what He does not initiate."

In Mueller's 70 years of ministry, the equivalent of *70 million dollars* ($70,000,000!) passed through his hands for his orphanages. In addition, another *35 million dollars* were expended by his Scriptural Knowledge Institute for the international distribution of Bibles, tracts and educational materials. Mueller housed, fed, clothed and educated as many as two thousand orphans at a time *without ever asking for a penny or even making his needs known.* God was the Provider for George Mueller!

For several years, Mueller was the sole supporter of Hudson Taylor's China mission — on one occasion giving a single contribution of 10 thousand British pounds, which is equivalent to 650 thousand dollars! In fact, over the course of his lifetime, Mueller's ministry *gave away* over 18 million dollars to missions. This was out of the overflow of God's abundant supply. His supply still overflows today.

Can we see how we have limited God by leaning so heavily on the help of man? Whether we go to the world for new fund raising ideas or merely put our trust in the monetary resources of believers, it is still leaning on the arm of flesh. "How often do we attempt work for God to the limit of our incompetency rather than to the limit of God's omnipotency" (Hudson Taylor). Why are we still holding Him back?

The silver and the gold are His. He will give us what we need if we follow His lead. His hand is not too short to save nor His ear too heavy to hear. He will supply if we will comply. God *will* fund His own work — abundantly. "We are asked to do an impossible task, but we work with Him who can do the impossible" (Taylor). *Let us give place to our supernatural Lord.*

It is time for us to cut the cord of worldly dependence and attach ourselves to the life support of God. Earthly methods will not produce heavenly fruit. Carnal techniques will not yield spiritual results. "Flesh gives birth to flesh, but the Spirit gives birth to spirit" (John 3:6). What is it we want to birth? Let us be jealous for the honor of our God and zealous for the purity of the gospel of our Messiah.

Is it wrong for ministries to make their needs known? Is it improper for them to share their visions and goals? Of course not, not at all! We are *all* fellow-workers with Him. We share together in His call. But there is absolutely no place for high-pressure tactics and passionate pleas, for marketing gimmicks and merchandising tricks, for slick salesmanship and manipulative methods — all done in the name of the Lord.

Jesus is about to spew this out of His mouth.

Chapter Eight

Whatever Happened To The Fear Of God?

America is ripe for judgment! Our selfish deeds have come up before the throne of God and we have been found sadly lacking. Our sinful lives have been weighed in the balance and we have come up pitifully short. Our preachers haven't clearly warned us, and our teachers haven't told us the whole truth. *Judgment is already in our land.*

Isaiah warned Jerusalem many years ago: "The Lord, the Lord Almighty, called you on that day to weep and wail, to tear out your hair and put on sackcloth. But see, there is joy and revelry, slaughtering of cattle and killing of sheep, eating of meat and drinking of wine! 'Let us eat and drink,' you say, 'for tomorrow we die!' " (Is. 22:12-13) Today we sing a new tune: "Let us eat and drink and be glad. America shall not die!" Little do we realize that the land of the free and the home of the brave is perishing before our eyes.

We are filled with an unreal optimism, not knowing that deterioration is already rampant in our culture. We sit smug and secure, proud and protected, but the divine axe has already been laid at the root of our society. We are too busy having fun and pursuing our dreams to even realize that America is falling apart.

Our nation is sick at heart. It reels from an ugly disease. *There is little justice in the land.* The American Bar Association, representing most of America's lawyers, officially came out pro-abortion. They are supposed to be *protecting* the innocent. "In Washington, D.C., within blocks of the Department of Justice, there are 37 'adult' bookstores, 8 X-rated theaters and 15 topless bars!" (cited by *Christ for the Nations Magazine*) Is it any wonder that our prisons are filled to overflowing, with more than *one million* people in jail? Recently the Pentagon's phone bill was audited. About 300 thousand dollars of our tax money was spent on Dial-a-Porn. Our national defense has exposed its soft underbelly! We are ready to be taken.

Then why aren't we busy repenting? Why are we hardly interceding for our land? Why are we so nonchalant and numb? *It is because we too have lost the fear of God.* Judgment has become an almost meaningless word. We have forgotten the Law of the Lord. But His holy standards have not changed.

"If your very own brother, or your son or daughter, or the wife you love, or your closest friend secretly entices you, saying, 'Let us go and worship other gods' . . . do not yield to him or listen to him. Show him no pity. Do not spare him or shield him. [Plea bargaining was entirely out of the question!] You must certainly put him to death. Your hand must be the first in putting him to death, and then the hands of all the people. Stone him to death, because he tried to turn you away from the Lord your God, who brought you out of Egypt, out of the land of slavery. *Then all Israel will hear and be afraid,* and no one among you will do such an evil thing again" (Deut. 13:6-11).

Yet America has birthed over *two thousand* false religions and idolatrous cults — including Mormonism, Christian Science, Jehovah's Witnesses and Scientology. Can we avoid the penalty of death?

Morality and honor used to be sacred. According to Israel's divine constitution, if a priest's daughter defiled herself by becoming a prostitute, she disgraced her father and *was to be burned in the fire* (Lev. 21:9). If there was a stubborn and rebellious son who would not obey his father and mother and would not listen to them when they disciplined him, they were to take him to the city elders and say: "This son of ours is stubborn and rebellious. He will not obey us. He is a profligate and a drunkard" (Deut. 21:20). Then all the men of his town would stone him to death. As the Lord clearly said, "You must purge the evil from among you. *All Israel will hear of it and be afraid*" (Deut. 21:21).

Today the exact opposite has occurred. (We don't need to start stoning adulterers again — but we've gone to the other extreme.) We have not purged the evil from our midst! Blatant sinners go unpunished; high-handed criminals walk away free. It is often the guilty who are protected by law. That's why America has not *heard* and is not *afraid*. That's why so many among us do evil things again and again.

Some judges have persecuted parents for home schooling their children while others have prevented parents from knowing that their own daughters are having abortions. In fact, those who protest abortion are jeered; those who practice abortion are cheered. Perversity has gripped our land! "Woe to those who call evil good and good evil, who put darkness for light and light for darkness, who put bitter for sweet and sweet for bitter" (Is. 5:20). Woe to the nation whose courts commit crimes! Recently, a two-time murderer was released on *two dollars* bail — only to kill again!

Do you know what the crime rate is in Saudi Arabia? Only 89 murders were committed in 1988. There were only 2563 acts of immorality (that's right — immorality is a criminal offence), 5312 cases of people making, selling, or drinking intoxicating beverages (this is enforced!), and a per-capita theft rate one-seventieth that of the United States. Why? Because adulterers are beheaded, drunkards are flogged, and thieves have their hands chopped off — in public, before the crowds! It is a regular weekly spectacle. The message is unmistakably clear. In this strict Muslim nation, breaking the law does not pay.

But in America we are trained the wrong way. (Don't think that I'm advocating Muslim law. *Enforcing* our own country's laws would be more than enough.) From our earliest days, we are taught that sin is okay and wrongdoing is relative. We do what is right in our own eyes. Even churches wince at the thought of discipline. We preach a great grandfather God. He is kindly and smiling and warm. He never gets indignant or angry. In His eyes we can do no wrong. He is blind to our sin and our guilt. But "grandfather" is not happy with this. He is awakening from His seeming slumber. His wrath is beginning to fall. He is not so blind after all.

What do the seven angels bring from the presence of God in Revelation, chapter 15?

> "Then one of the four living creatures gave to the seven angels seven golden bowls filled with the wrath of God, who lives for ever and ever. . . . Then I heard a loud voice from

the temple saying to the seven angels, 'Go, pour out the seven bowls of God's wrath on the earth' " (Rev. 15:7, 16:1).

And after the seven bowls are poured out, the Son of God will appear, "revealed from heaven in blazing fire" (2 Thess. 1:7). We are beginning to feel the heat.

Here is a frightful thought. *Every sin that is not under the blood must be punished.* Every transgression must be judged. God has a record of every abortion, every rape, every theft, every murder, every lie, every injustice, every blasphemy, every adulterous affair, every homosexual union, every pornographic act, every satanic ritual, every godless sermon — every single sin that has ever been committed in our country. He remembers all the cries of the helpless little children who have been abused, of the terrified wives who have been beaten, of the destitute poor who have been forgotten. Think of how much divine wrath has accumulated for our land! *The containers of judgment are brimming.*

Our "anything-goes" gospel has put us to sleep. We have been sadly deceived! But "God cannot be mocked. A man reaps what he sows [this holds true for a nation as well]. The one who sows to please his sinful nature, from that nature will reap destruction; the one who sows to please the Spirit, from the Spirit will reap eternal life" (Gal. 6:7-8). We have sowed to please our sinful nature. We are beginning to reap destruction. The day of accounting is here!

This is what God said to Israel:
"Do not defile yourselves in any of these ways [incest, bestiality, homosexuality, adultery], because this is how the nations that I am going to drive out before you became defiled. *Even the land was defiled, so I punished it for its sin, and the land vomited out its inhabitants"* (Lev. 18:24-25).
Yet such sins are rampant in our country. Organizations promoting incest have been formed (one group says that sexual

activity must begin before the age of *eight* — otherwise it's too late!). Even bestiality has been captured on a best-selling porno film. Who says our land won't vomit us out? If God could destroy the Canaanites for these abominations (the Canaanites had no Bible!), can't He destroy us?

"Do not pollute the land where you are. *Bloodshed pollutes the land*, and atonement cannot be made for the land on which blood has been shed, except by the blood of the one who shed it. *Do not defile the land* where you live and where I dwell, for I, the Lord, dwell among the Israelites [does His Spirit dwell among us today?]" (Num. 35:33-34).

But with garbage cans overflowing with the torn-up bodies of aborted babies, and our city streets stained with the blood of the slain, our very future hangs precariously in the balance.

"The sin of the house of Israel and Judah is exceedingly great; *the land is full of bloodshed and the city is full of injustice.* They say, 'The Lord has forsaken the land; the Lord does not see.' So I will not look on them with pity or spare them, but I will bring down on their own heads what they have done" (Ezek. 9:9-10). God's judgment had finally come.

How awful it would have been for America under Old Testament law! But now, in the period of grace, the ultimate penalties have become much more extreme. "Anyone who rejected the law of Moses died without mercy on the testimony of two or three witnesses. How much more severely do you think a man deserves to be punished who has trampled the Son of God under foot, who has treated as an unholy thing the blood of the covenant that sanctified him, and who has insulted the Spirit of grace?" (Heb. 10:28-29) *Let us tremble with fear for our land.* The kindness of God has been spurned.

So much light has been given to us. How much obedience will be required of us? So much knowledge has been imparted to us. How much responsibility lies at our feet? "If they did not escape when they refused Him who warned them on earth, how much less will we, if we turn away from Him who warns us from heaven. For if the message spoken by angels was binding, and every violation and disobedience received its just punishment, how shall we escape if we ignore so great a salvation? It is a dreadful thing to fall into the hands of the living God."

Has America fallen too far?

Chapter Nine

The Prosperity Trap

All of us have read the Parable of the Sower. A farmer went out to sow his seed. (His seed was the Word of God.) Some of the seed "fell along the path, and the birds came and ate it up" (Mark 4:4). This represents those who hear the message about the kingdom and do not understand it. Immediately "Satan comes and takes away the word that was sown in them" (Mark 4:15). It never really entered their hearts.

Some seed "fell on rocky places, where it did not have much soil. It sprang up quickly, because the soil was shallow. But when the sun came up, the plants were scorched, and they withered because they had no root" (Mark 4:5-6). This stands for those "who hear the word and at once receive it with joy. But since they have no root, they last only a short time. When trouble or persecution comes because of the word, they quickly fall away" (Mark 4:16-17). Yet these people knew the Lord!

Look carefully at what the Scriptures say: the people whose hearts are like rocky soil hear the Word, and at once *receive it with joy*. Luke tells us that "*they believe for a while*, but in the time of testing they fall away" (Luke 8:13) — because they have no root! It is not because they reject the message. It is not because they do not believe. *It is because they have no depth.* Their commitment is only skin deep. When pressures mount, when troubles arise, when persecutions come, their whole walk with God collapses. This is a picture of many of us!

Let's be honest with ourselves. If real persecution came our way, most of us would cave in. We would deny the Lord! We're not being faithful in the little, how can we expect to be faithful in the big? If we succumb to peer pressure and the fear of man *now,* when our homes and jobs are not at stake, how will we fare then, when our very lives may be on the line? "For if men do these things when the tree is green, what will happen when it is dry?" (Luke 23:31)

We are deceiving ourselves if we think that one day we will boldly proclaim Jesus as Lord — even at gun point under threat of death — when today we deny Him because we fear offending our in-laws or neighbors. How will we pass the great test when we consistently fail the small tests? If we are always falling into Satan's little snares for our lives — those nagging "minor" sins and everyday temptations — we can not expect to resist the devil's all out final assault.

Remember: the condition of the shallow-hearted hearers was only fully revealed when trouble and persecution came. What "heart condition" will be revealed in us when real testings arise? "If you have raced with foot men and they have worn you out, how can you compete with horses? If you stumble in safe country, how will you manage in the thickets by the Jordan?" (Jer. 12:5) Now is the time to deepen our walk. Now is the time to fortify our faith. We cannot afford to wait and see!

And then there is the seed sown among thorns "which grew up and choked the plants, so that they did not bear grain" (Mark 4:7). This represents those who hear the Word, but the worries of this life, the deceitfulness of wealth, and the desires for other things come in and "choke the word, making it unfruitful" (Mark 4:19). *What an illustration this is of a great part of the American church!*

There are so many thorns all around us: the worries of this life, the pleasures of this world, the deceitfulness of wealth, and the desire for other things. Because of these thorns, most of us "do not mature" and the Word in us becomes unfruitful (Luke 8:14; Mark 4:19). Just think of what our lives would be like if these thorns were removed! There would be no more anxiety about finances or our earthly security; no more seeking fulfillment from worldly pleasures; no more putting our trust in money or living for material gain; no more being motivated by outside desires — by the insatiable drive to be someone, to have something, to go somewhere, to find our satisfaction everywhere but in Jesus.

But the American Church not only lives among thorns, we preach a "thorny" gospel! We tell worldly minded people that following Jesus is the path to success. "If you walk with the Lord," we say, "He will make you wealthy!" *But that is not the gospel.* "Take up your cross" does not mean "become rich and famous." "Leave everything and follow Me" is not the same as "get everything by following Me." We are catering our gospel to carnality!

Jesus said, "Do not be afraid, little flock, for your Father has been pleased to give you the kingdom. [This verse is often quoted to prove that God wants all of us to be rich! But that's not what Jesus said. Let's keep on reading.] *Sell your possessions and give to the poor.* Provide purses for yourselves that will not wear out, a treasure in heaven that will not be exhausted, where no thief comes near and no moth destroys. For where your treasure is, there your heart will be also" (Luke 12:32-34). Where are our treasures being stored?

It is *because* our Father has been pleased to give us the kingdom that we can freely sell our possessions and give to the poor. "For the kingdom of God is not a matter of eating and drinking, but of righteousness, peace, and joy in the Holy Spirit" (Rom. 14:17). We have it backwards! We say, "*Because* our Father, the King, has given us the kingdom, we ought to start living like King's kids now! Let's not sell our possessions; let's accumulate more possessions!" We act as if the kingdom of God *were* a matter of eating and drinking, of wanting and having, of fancy cars and luxurious homes, of big bank accounts and expensive designer clothes. We have lost sight of the object of our faith — Jesus, the Son of God.

Oh yes, God can and will supply all our needs — and there is nothing shabby about His provisions. He is not glorified through our poverty and lack, nor does He gain anything when we grovel in debt. He is a God of infinite wealth and He can afford to share it with us. *All* that we need is found in Him. When we seek His kingdom first, He will provide for us. But God "will not aid men in their selfish striving after personal gain. He will not help men to attain ends which, when attained, usurp the place He by every right should hold in their interest and affection" (A. W. Tozer). Material wealth is never to be our goal.

Paul could not possibly have warned us more clearly: "People who *want to get rich* fall into temptation and a trap and into many foolish and harmful desires that plunge men into ruin and destruction. For the *love of money* is a root of all kinds of evil. Some people, *eager for money,* have wandered from the faith and pierced themselves with many griefs" (1 Tim. 6:9-10). Let us not read these verses lightly. Our very salvation could be at stake. Paul speaks of "temptation and a trap," of being plunged into "ruin and destruction," of "all kinds of evil," of "wandering from the faith."

And so Paul exhorted Timothy in no uncertain terms:

"But you man of God, *flee from all this* [today we run after it!] and pursue righteousness, godliness, faith, love, endurance and gentleness. For godliness with contentment is great gain. For we brought nothing into the world, and we can take nothing out of it. But if we have food and clothing, we will be content with that" (6:11,6-8).

But are we really content? Or are we like the Pharisees who loved money and sneered at Jesus when He taught against greed (Luke 16:14)?

The Book of Proverbs says that "there are three things that are never satisfied, four that never say, 'Enough!': the grave, the barren womb, land, which is never satisfied with water, and fire, which never says 'Enough!' " (30:15-16) Today we can add one more: the materialistic American Church! We are like the two daughters of the leech who cry "Give! Give!" (Prov. 30:15). We never have enough!

This is what has happened to our modern-day prosperity gospel: *It has run aground on the shallow shores of greed and ambition, it has capsized in the turbulent waters of selfishness, it has sunk under the weight of covetous hearts.* May it never sail again!

How could we be so blind? We have encouraged people to "want to get rich." We have told them that it is all right to be "eager for money." We have taught carnally-minded believers, who have not died to the world, to pursue worldly wealth. We have tried to make the whole thing so spiritual, as if the reason God exists is to meet all our wants. Some even teach: "You can have whatever you say, so just speak it out all the time — a swimming pool, a giant screen TV, a mink stole. The Lord wants you to have an abundant life!" And now many of us are trapped. We have taken our eyes off Jesus and put them on earthly treasures. The deceitfulness of wealth has tricked us again. It has stolen eternity from our hearts! Some of us have even become *fools*— we have stored up things for ourselves but are not rich toward God (Luke 12:20-21).

Two thousand years ago, Jesus sounded an alarm: "Watch out! *Be on your guard against all kinds of greed;* a man's life does not consist in the abundance of his possessions" (Luke 12:15). Yet today we glorify greed and sanctify selfishness under the guise of great faith. We measure heavenly blessing by earthly bounty and equate real spirituality with financial success. Have we forgotten that "God has chosen those who are poor in the eyes of the world to be rich in faith and to inherit the kingdom He promised those who love Him" (James 2:5)? Do we realize that "what is highly valued among men is detestable in God's sight" (Luke 16:15)? It is the man who lives for riches who "will fade away even while he goes about his business" (James 1:11). Let us cleanse our hearts now of all covetousness!

James accused his readers of being adulterous people, friends with the world. This was one of their symptoms: "When you ask, you do not receive, because you ask with wrong motives, *that you may spend what you get on your pleasures*" (James 4:3). Yet our new teaching has fostered such praying! We have given it biblical support! Today we really know how to "use the Word" — to get new cars and diamond rings! *And we actually think all this is spiritual.* God have mercy on us!

There is so much idolatry in our midst. How much longer can we survive? Paul said that a greedy person is an idolater, and that idolaters do not enter the kingdom of God (Eph. 5:5). Are we selling our inheritance for a piece of bread?

No, there is nothing wrong with having possessions. But there *is* something wrong with possessions having us! There is nothing wrong with being rich — as long as being rich is not the purpose of our being! We cannot serve both God and money (Matt. 6:24).

Here is something to consider. Idolatry has taken on a new twist in our day. People who would never even put a portrait of Jesus on their walls for fear of having a graven image now put pictures of BMW's on their refrigerators so they can see them all the time. They are believing God for a new set of wheels! They have graduated from the "Cadillac kind of faith" and moved right into "foreign-sports-car confession." They think they have become giants in the Lord. But they are sadly mistaken. Maybe God has given them over to their "spiritual lusts." The true faith giants have their eyes on eternity. In heaven we walk on gold!

Let's carefully consider our motives. We ask God for an abundance of funds so that we can help to spread the gospel worldwide, yet only the tiniest fraction of our income is given to reaching the lost. Has it ever occurred to us to live on less (that's right, to sacrifice!) so that we might have more to give? Could this be the New Testament gospel? We boast about our tithing. But for many of us it is simply a good financial investment. We give ten percent for the sake of our wallets, not for the sake of the work. Sure we love the Lord. But we love what He can do for us even more. That's what it means to be blessed! What if our "hundred fold" return came in the form of many souls being saved? Would we somehow feel shortchanged? How deeply have we died to this world? Let us examine our hearts and take stock of our lives. This is our chance to be free.

How then do we live among thorns? What must we do to avoid being choked? Listen again to the words of Paul:

"Command those who are rich in this present world [that applies to almost *all* Americans!] not to be arrogant nor to put their hope in wealth, which is so uncertain, but to put their hope in God, who richly provides us with everything for our enjoyment. Command them to do good, to be rich in good deeds, and to be generous and willing to share. In this way they will lay up treasure for themselves as a firm foundation for the coming age, so that they may take hold of the life that is truly life" (1 Tim. 6:17-19). That is fulfillment in Him!

There is still hope for each of us in the Word. We can uproot the thorn bushes and pull out the weeds. We can make our soil healthy and sound. And we can bear fruit for the Lord. There is seed sown on *good soil* too! This "stands for those with a noble and good heart, who hear the word, retain it, and by persevering produce a crop . . . [multiplying] thirty, sixty, or even a hundred times what was sown" (Luke 8:15; Mark 4:20).

May *this* be our story and song.

Chapter Ten

Jesus The Radical

Jesus was completely different from any one who ever walked the earth. He was totally holy, righteous and just — absolutely free from all sin. He was totally pure, loving and merciful, without a hint of malice or venom. He was full of God and empty of ambition — the image of the heavenly, yet clothed with the earthly. *And, according to the standards of this world, He was totally radical.* That's why He was nailed to a cross. Sinful man couldn't stand His light. His gaze still unnerves us today. It is not always easy to look Him in the eye.

Consider the Son of God.

Jesus never did anything to be seen by men. He lived for His Father alone. Human praise didn't motivate Him. Human criticism didn't move Him. Fame had no meaning to Him at all. Wanting to please His Father, He cared only for Heaven's smile. But the religious hypocrites were different: *"Everything they do is done for men to see"* (Matt. 23:5) — just like so many of us!

How would we act if no human eyes were watching us or would ever know our lives? Would we sin more? Would we serve less? Who do we resemble more — Jesus or the hypocrites?

The hypocrites loved to give to the needy in public and to pray standing in the synagogues and on the street corners — *to be seen and admired by men.* They loved to be given the place of honor at banquets and the most important seats in public services — *to be exalted in the sight of men.* They loved to be recognized as spiritual leaders and to be greeted with lofty titles — *to be acclaimed and respected by men* — just like so many of us!

We love to be invited to sit on the platform or to have our anointing acknowledged by the crowds. We are thrilled when the big names know who we are — maybe one day they'll even ask us to speak.

But Jesus saw the folly of it all. He knew what really mattered. Only His Father's approval was important. If God was pleased then the case was closed. There was no need for discussion or prayer. Heaven's word alone carried weight. He refused to be moved by mere flesh and blood. "As for man, his days are like grass, he flourishes like a flower of the field; the wind blows over it and it is gone, and its place remembers it no more. . . . but the word of our God stands forever" (Ps. 103:15-16; Is. 40:8). In the light of eternity, how big is man? One word of God will outlast all the human empires that have ever been built.

Yet we are so often moved by the opinions of others! We work for human approval more than divine approval. We take counsel with man more than we take counsel with God. We keep our earthly appointments but break our heavenly appointments. People come first, prayer comes last (if it comes at all!). We value the companionship of friends more than the communion of our Friend — at least that's what our schedules say! How often do we set aside a whole day or night *to spend just with the Lord?* Yet we spend so much time with one another!

But Jesus didn't live like that at all. He had enjoyed unbroken fellowship with His Father before He came into this world. No human being could rob Him of that union. He was determined to walk with His God whatever the consequences or cost. "The One who sent Me is with Me; He has not left Me alone, for I always do what please Him" (John 8:29).

Jesus had a completely different perspective than we do. He *came down* from heaven to earth. He had created the moon and the sun. He had fashioned and shaped every star. The galaxies were the work of His hands. Holy angels fell in awe at His feet. He could rightly evaluate man. No mortal could boast in His sight.

One day "the arrogance of man will be brought low and the pride of men [will be] humbled" (Is. 2:17). One day "men will flee to caves in the rocks and to holes in the ground from dread of the Lord and the splendor of His majesty" (Is. 2:19). One day God Himself will rise to shake the earth, and all mankind will tremble. Will anyone boast on that day when the King makes the *whole world* quake? "Oh, cease to glorify man, who has only a breath in his nostrils! For by what does he merit esteem?" (Is. 2:22, New Jewish Version)

Jesus lived in the light of the Judgment. He knew that *everything* would one day be revealed. Hypocrisy was utterly pointless. There was no reason to put on an act because it would all come out one day. The *whole truth* would then be uncovered. This is what Jesus taught:

"There is nothing concealed that will not be disclosed, or hidden that will not be made known. What you have said in the dark will be heard in the daylight, and what you have whispered in the ear in the inner rooms will be proclaimed from the roofs" (Luke 12:2-3).

These are sobering words! Will that Day bring us glory or shame?

"Those iniquities which men hide in their hearts shall be written one day on their foreheads as with the point of a diamond" (Thomas Watson). And everyone will be there to see! We may fool a few people now, but we will be exposed before all on that Day.

Living in the reality of that great divine disclosure can free us from all outward displays. It can make us disciples in deed and in truth. It can help us live in true holy fear. God's records do not lie! "Nothing in all creation is hidden from God's sight. Everything is uncovered and laid bare before the eyes of Him *to whom we must give account*" (Heb. 4:13). He will set things straight.

George Whitefield, the great British evangelist, was often falsely accused and maligned. The clergy spoke out against him, artists painted mocking portraits of his meetings, and slanderous tracts were published to attack him. But when his friends urged him to defend himself against the lies he refused. "I am content to wait till the judgment day," he said, "for the clearing up of my character. When I am dead I desire no epitaph but this, 'Here lies G. W. What kind of man he was the great day will discover.' " He had committed himself to the Lord. He was looking beyond this world.

"Though [Whitefield] wrote *Journals* of his ministry during its first three years, he thereafter refused to take any steps towards making a correct knowledge of his life available. With his eye fixed on his accounting in heaven, he sought no justification of himself on earth" (Arnold Dallimore). What a contrast with the hypocrites who justified themselves in the sight of men — but God knew their hearts (Luke 16:15). *And He knows our hearts too.*

That's why Paul told us never to judge a man's inner motives. "Wait till the Lord comes," he said. "He will bring to light what is hidden in darkness and will expose the motives of men's hearts. At that time each will receive his praise from God" (1 Cor. 4:5). On that Day, the first will be last and the last will be first, and *everything* will be made right — forever. On that Day, many eyes will be opened and many mouths will be closed. If we can be content to wait until then, God's "Well done!" will be worth it all.

Jesus always walked in this truth. *He never sought the praises of men.* In fact, He would not even *accept* praise from men (John 5:41). He knew how fickle human beings could be. One day they shouted, "Hail to the King!", and the next day they cried, "Crucify Him!" One moment the crowds wanted to own Him; the next moment they tried to stone Him.

But God's evaluation is based on truth, and "no one can change God's opinion about you except you" (Leonard Ravenhill). Popularity polls do not affect Him. Surveys do not influence Him. He knows who He esteems: the one who is humble and contrite in spirit, and trembles at His Word (Is. 66:2). With *him* the Father is pleased. For performers He has no place.

The religious hypocrites had it all wrong. Their priorities were completely reversed. They believed, but they would not act, "for they loved praise from men more than praise from God" (John 12:43). Their man-centered orientation paralyzed their faith. They were moved by what they could see. And so, for *this life only,* they impressed flesh and blood, but they made no impression on heaven. They received their reward in full here on earth — and lost the reward that counts forever. What a pitiful, pathetic choice!

Yet it is a choice we often make. If the truth were known today, many of us would be exposed as lovers of the praise of men more than lovers of the praise of God. We would have to confess that we have held ourselves back many times — even when we believed that it was God Himself who was prompting us — so as not to lose the esteem of our peers. But this is a great deception because *our peers want our esteem as well.* How foolish all of this is!

The Corinthians were impressed with people. They loved to follow man. But Paul had to straighten them out:

"What, after all, is Apollos? [Remember, Apollos was quite a powerful preacher!] And what is Paul? [Paul was the mightiest apostle who ever lived!] *Only servants,* through whom you came to believe — as the Lord has assigned to each his task. I planted the seed, Apollos watered it, *but God* made it grow. So neither he who plants nor he who he waters is anything, but *only God,* who makes things grow. . . . So then, *no more boasting about men!*" (1 Cor. 3:5-7,21)

And may flattery perish as well: *"for if I were skilled in flattery, my Maker would soon take me away"* (Job 32:21-22).

But we are always lifting up men! We are like the followers of Whitefield who wanted him to perpetuate his memory by forming a denomination under his name. They were concerned that others would get credit for his work. But his reply was always the same: "No, let the name of Whitefield die, so that the cause of Jesus Christ may live . . . Let the name of Whitefield perish, but Christ be glorified . . . I have had enough popularity to be sick of it." May we learn to be sick of it too! A glimpse into eternity would cure us of our shortsightedness.

Paul gave up everything to follow the Lord. He totally died to this world. His heart was set on one thing: "we make it our goal to please Him" (2 Cor. 5:9). In that there could be no compromise. The choice was either-or. "Am I now trying to win the approval *of men, or of God? Or am I trying to please men? If I were still trying to please man, I would not be a servant of Christ"* (Gal. 1:10). He decisively submitted to God. The world has been changed since that day.

What would have happened to Jesus' ministry if He pleased His disciples or the religious leaders or the crowds? He would have completely missed His Father's will. He would never have been crucified. His blood would never have been shed. And He would never have told us the truth. No one would have wanted to hear it! *We would not be saved today if Jesus had been a pleaser of men.*

But there are many churches in our land that are being ruined by a man-pleasing spirit. The leaders are pursuing the crowd when they are supposed to be following the cloud. They are experts in bringing in the people but novices in bringing down the power. Rather than cultivating faith, they are courting favor. They want to be in tune with the sheep, but they have gotten out of harmony with the Shepherd. And *He* knows what is good for the flock. Doing things His way is life. The pastor who walks in *His* footsteps will truly serve the sheep.

We must build according to His heavenly pattern. Only then will He dwell in our midst (Ex. 25:8-9). Twelve Spirit-shaped radicals could do more to turn our society right side up than twelve million man-made replicas. But we are reproducing disciples of man. They lack conviction and have no back bone. They are spineless and easily swayed. (Some have tried to compensate for this in the flesh and have become proud and over-bearing). How we need Messiah's image in our lives!

"Here is the reason why we have such a host of stillborn, sinewless, ricketty, powerless spiritual children. They are *born of half-dead* parents, a sort of sentimental religion which does not take hold of the soul, which has no depth of earth, no grasp, no power in it, and the result is a sickly crop of sentimental converts. Oh! the Lord give us a real, robust, living, hardy, Christianity, full of zeal and faith, which shall bring into the kingdom of God lively, well-developed children, full of life and energy, instead of these poor sentimental ghosts that are hopping around us" (Catherine Booth).

Religious hypocrites suffer from a crippling disease: the chronic fear of man. It is an utterly debilitating condition that undermines obedience and faith. How often we too are stricken with it — whether we are hypocrites or not! *We are intimidated by man.* How many moves of God have been cut short by a man fearing spirit? "But what will *the people* say?"

The fear of man is a snare (Prov. 29:25); it is so easy to be caught in it. King Saul had a commission from the Lord, but he "was afraid of the people and so [he] gave in to them" (1 Sam. 15:24). He had one eye on God and the other eye on man. Because he was double minded and unstable at heart, he lost both the flock and God's favor. He forfeited the kingship to another. God wanted a man after His heart.

It was because of the fear of man that:
Joseph of Arimathea was only a *secret* disciple (John 19:38);
people would not say anything publicly about Jesus (John 7:13);
Peter denied the Lord (Matt. 26:69-74);
the parents of the blind man who was healed would not acknowledge the miracle (John 9:22); and
the disciples met together behind closed doors before they knew that the Lord had risen (John 20:19).

But Jesus Himself knew no fear. He would not give place to its lies. He knew who was to be feared. It surely was not man! "Do not be afraid of those who kill the body but cannot kill the soul. Rather, be afraid of the One who can destroy both body and soul in hell" (Matt. 10:28). A healthy fear of God will drive all other fears away. And *"the man who is intimate with God will never be intimidated by man"* (Ravenhill). Intimacy with God is the key.

When saintly John Fletcher died in 1786, his wife said this of him: "It was his constant endeavor to maintain an uninterrupted sense of the presence of God. . . . Indeed, he both acted, and spoke, and thought, as under the eye of God. And thus setting God always before him, he remained unmoved in all occurrences . . . Sometimes he took his journeys alone; but above a thousand miles I have traveled with him; during which neither change of company, place, nor the variety of circumstances which naturally occur in traveling ever seemed to make the least difference in his firm attention to the presence of God. . . . And I can say with truth, all his union with me was so intermingled with prayer and praise that every employment and every meal was, as it were, perfumed therewith."

This was what made Jesus different: He lived every second with His Father. He stayed in the presence of God. He walked in unceasing communion. The Two were entirely One. Abba was His intimate Friend.

But intimacy with God carries a price . . .

Chapter Eleven

The Baptism Of Tears

More than anything else in this world, God wants us to share His heart. We are often hungry for His power, but seldom aware of His pain. We are eager to experience His goodness, but think little of His grief. "Our Lord still agonizes for souls" (John Hyde). This must be at the foundation of our lives. Jesus bears our burdens. Can we bear His as well?

Most of us are hardened to the needs of our suffering race. We are rarely touched by its cry. But this world is filled with dying — every second there is a sigh. Pain and sickness, tragedy and despair — God's creation is wasting away. Does our Father turn a deaf ear?

"A prisoner in a Romanian underground solitary cell was horrified at the cries of those tortured around him. He begged God for a little respite in heaven: 'Take me there at least for a little while.'

"Happily, he began to soar higher and higher, hoping soon to hear angelic music. But the closer he came to heaven, the louder became the cries of suffering. When he reached his goal it had become unbearable.

"He asked God, 'Is heaven not a place of serenity?'

"He was told, 'You seem never to have been attentive to what you read. It is written that the cries of oppressed slaves came up to Me, and I heard them (Exodus 2:23,24). The blood of Abel cries out to Me (Genesis 4:15).'

" 'Those with Me in heaven also hear this cry and that of all the innocents who are slain.'

" 'In your cell you hear the groanings of only a few. In heaven we hear the weeping of all who suffer.'

" 'Jesus represented Me by becoming a Man of Sorrows, acquainted with grief (Isaiah 53:3).'

" 'Read again about Rachel, who wept when children were killed in Bethlehem. Saints here weep with all who weep' " (Richard Wurmbrand). Can we hear the heart of this story without arguing about its theology?

In the Beatitudes, Jesus taught us to be like Him. That is the place of blessedness. If we share His nature, we will be poor in spirit and pure of heart, meek as well as merciful. We will be peacemakers and we will be persecuted. We will be hungry and thirsty for righteousness. *And we will mourn.* "Blessed are those who mourn, for they will be comforted" (Matt. 5:4). "Blessed are you who weep now, for you will laugh" (Luke 6:21).

There *is* a time for joy and there is a time for laughter. But there is also a time for mourning, and there is a time for weeping too. Our contemporary Church needs to learn how to weep!

"One of the things we need is a baptism of tears. A baptism of tears for the lethargic state of our life, and the curse our souls have tolerated. My how the church needs to confess! . . . Think of Jesus Christ coming to the world after these hundreds of years and finding the church asleep and the people dying in the toils of suffering!" (John G. Lake) How we need a sensitive heart!

We speak of our relationship with the Lord. But relationship means sharing. Relationship means one heart. Relationship means mutual joy. And relationship means mutual pain. Do we have a *relationship* with the Lord?

"He who unites himself with the Lord is one with Him in spirit" (1 Cor. 6:17). This was the agony of the prophets. They carried the burden of God and participated in the pain of their people:

"Streams of tears flow from my eyes, for Your law is not obeyed" (Ps. 119:136).

"Turn away from me, let me weep bitterly. Do not try and console me over the destruction of my people" (Is. 22:4).

"Oh, my anguish, my anguish! I writhe in pain. Oh, the agony of my heart! . . . Since my people are crushed, I am crushed; I mourn and horror grips me. . . . Oh, that my head were a spring of water and my eyes a fountain of tears! I would weep day and night for the slain of my people" (Jer. 4:19, 8:21, 9:1).

"I have great sorrow and unceasing anguish in my heart. For I could wish I myself were cursed and cut off from Christ for the sake of my brothers, those of my own race" (Rom. 9:2-3)

Does the Son of God hurt any less?

"As He approached Jerusalem and saw the city, He wept over it. . . . O Jerusalem, Jerusalem, you who kill the prophets and stone those sent to you, *how often I have longed to gather your children, as a hen gathers her chicks under her wings,* but you were not willing" (Luke 19:41; Matt. 23:37).

The baptism of tears is a baptism into the suffering of the Lord. It is a participation in His afflictions. As He was — and is — rejected, we are rejected. As He was — and is — despised, we too are despised. And as His heart was — and is — broken, ours

is broken as well. *There is great intimacy in sharing His heart.*
This was the apostle's desire: "I want to know Christ and the
power of His resurrection and *the fellowship of sharing in His
sufferings,* becoming like Him in His death" (Phil. 3:10). There is
no higher calling than that.

We so desperately try to attain happiness in life. We make
every effort to enhance our well being. The gospel of suffering is
foreign to us: We hardly know how to pour out our lives. Our
capacity for true love is lacking. Compassion is too costly for us.
We are complacent in the midst of great anguish. We are distant
from the pains of the world. But God hears every cry and sees
every tear. Each life is precious in His sight. What heartache our
Father must feel! God, who is Love, must know grief.

There is a night I will never forget. It was the end of a
two-and-a-half year struggle. We were fighting for the life of a
dear brother who was stricken with an incurable disease. We
had fasted and prayed and battled. We had seen miraculous
breakthroughs — even his doctors were amazed. But now the
end had come, and there was nothing we could do. While we
worshiped and interceded, his breathing stopped. He was cut
down before his time, and none of us could bring him back.

We watched with sobs as his wife cast herself on his lifeless
body, caressing his face, soaking him with her tears. The two of
them were just thirty-five years old, their two girls only twelve
and ten. All their best years were yet to come. And now he was
gone from this life.

The next day we sat and cried with their little daughter. "I
want my daddy, I want my daddy. I wish this never happened. I
told mommy that I wish the nightmare would be over." But her
mother could only say, "The nightmare will be over when Jesus
comes back. Then you'll see daddy again."

My God, the needs are great! How can we live without tears? Where is our heart of compassion? How can we be so selfish? Why do we hold ourselves back?

"A man with leprosy came to [Jesus] and begged Him on his knees, 'If you are willing, you can make me clean.' *Filled with compassion,* Jesus reached out His hand and touched the man. 'I am willing,' He said. 'Be clean!' " (Mark 1:40-41)

"When He saw the crowds, *He had compassion on them,* because they were harassed and helpless, like sheep without a shepherd" (Matt. 9:36).

When Jesus saw the funeral procession carrying a widow's dead son, *He was moved with compassion for her* and He said, " 'Don't cry.' Then He went up and touched the coffin, and those carrying it stood still. He said, 'Young man, I say to you, get up!' The dead man sat up and began to talk, and Jesus gave him back to his mother" (Luke 7:12-15). Oh, for the compassion of the Lord!

Once Smith Wigglesworth was called to the bedside of a young woman who was dying of tuberculosis. He insisted that the distraught family leave the room.

"I knew," he said, "that God would move nothing in an atmosphere of mere natural sympathy and unbelief." He knelt down and began to pray. "Then," he continued, "the fight came."

"It seemed as though the heavens were brass. I prayed from eleven to three-thirty in the morning. I saw the glimmering light on the face of the sufferer and saw her pass away. The devil said, 'Now you are done for. You have come from Bradford and the girl has died on your hands.' I said, 'It can't be. God did not send me here for nothing. This is a time to change strength.' I remembered that passage which said,

'Men ought always to pray and not to faint.' Death had taken place, but I knew that my God was all powerful and He that had split the Red Sea is just the same today. It was a time when I would not have no, and God said yes. I looked at the window and at that moment the face of Jesus appeared. It seemed as though a million rays of light were coming from His face. As He looked at the one who had just passed away, the color came back to the face. She rolled over and fell asleep. Then I had a glorious time. In the morning she woke early, put on a dressing gown and walked to the piano. She started to play and to sing a wonderful song. The mother and the sister and the brother came down to listen. The Lord had undertaken. A miracle had been wrought."

What was the key? "You and I will never do anything except on the line of compassion. We shall never be able to remove the cancer until we are immersed so deeply into the power of the Holy Spirit, that the compassion of Christ is moving through us. . . . It is as your heart goes out to the needy ones in deep compassion that the Lord manifests His presence. . . . There is a fruit of the Spirit that must accompany the gift of healing, and that is longsuffering. The man who is going through with God, to be used in healing must be a man of longsuffering" (Wigglesworth). But compassion does not come without sacrifice. "It seems to me that until God has mowed you down, you never can have this longsuffering for others" (Wigglesworth). Are we willing to let God mow us down? There must be an emptying of our lives if God is to be our all in all.

"If the church ever succeeds in doing that which God purposes we should we do, it can only be when we enter into that divine compassion of the Son of God" (John G. Lake). In fact, this was the active force behind our very redemption: "The greatest movement in the soul of God was that movement of compassion for a needy world. It was so great that the Word says, 'For God so loved the world that He gave His only begotten Son . . . ' " (Lake). As we pour ourselves out, God's love is poured in.

Listen to the words of Uggo Bassi:
"Measure thy life by loss instead of gain,
Not by the wine drunk, but the wine poured forth;
For love's strength standeth in love's sacrifice,
And whoso suffers most hath most to give."
How much do we have to give?

No, God does not want us to be morbid, to go about sullen and downcast. We are not to expect senseless tragedy; we are not to roll over and die. But God *does* want us to feel His feelings. Jesus still says, "Follow Me."

Evan Roberts carried an intense burden for Wales. He pleaded for one hundred thousand souls. He entered into the intercessory life of the risen Lord. He experienced true agony of heart. Here is a description of this period of Robert's life, written by Evan Phillips, a man who had been involved in the 1859 Welsh Revival and was now part of the 1904 Revival:
"Evan Roberts was like a particle of radium in our midst. Its fire was consuming and felt abroad as something which took away sleep, cleared the channel of tears, and sped the golden wheels of prayer throughout the area . . . I did not weep much in the 1859 revival, but I have wept now until my heart is supple. In the midst of the greatest tearfulness I have found the greatest joy. I had felt for a year or two that there was a sighing of the wind, and something whispered that the storm could not be far away. Soon I felt the waters begin to cascade. Now the bed belongs to the river and Wales belong to Christ."

The river of tears overflowed its banks, and it was with weeping such as that the one hundred thousand were won. For "weeping may remain for a night, but rejoicing comes in the morning" (Ps. 30:5), and it is only those who share His pain who can truly share His joy. *In the kingdom, godly sorrow and godly joy go hand in hand.*

Paul was "sorrowful, yet always rejoicing" (2 Cor. 6:10).

Jesus, the Man of sorrows, was anointed with the oil of joy above His companions (Heb. 1:9).

"Those who sow with tears will reap with songs of joy. He who goes out weeping, carrying seed to sow, will return with songs of joy, carrying sheaves with him" (Ps. 126:5-6).

Oh, for the baptism of tears!

Chapter Twelve

The Gospel Of Suffering

If there is one thing that we can expect here as followers of Jesus, it is suffering.

"*In this world you shall have trouble. But take heart! I have overcome the world*" (John 16:33).

"*We must go through many hardships* to enter the kingdom of God" (Acts 14:22).

"Now if we are children, then we are heirs — heirs of God and co-heirs with Christ, *if indeed we share in His sufferings* in order that we may also share in His glory" (Rom. 8:17).

"I, John, your brother and companion in *the suffering and kingdom and patient endurance* that are ours in Jesus" (Rev. 1:9).

"And the God of all grace, Who called you to His eternal glory in Christ, *after you have suffered a little while*, will Himself restore you and make you strong, firm and steadfast" (1 Pet. 5:10).

Suffering for the Lord is a privilege:

"For it has been granted to you on behalf of Christ not only to believe on Him, but also to suffer for Him" (Phil. 1:29).

Suffering for Him is a joy:

"We rejoice in the hope of the glory of God . . . [and] we also *rejoice* in our sufferings" (Rom. 5:2-3).

"*Rejoice* in that day [when you are hated and excluded because of Jesus] and *leap for joy,* because great is your reward in heaven" (Luke 6:23).

"Dear friends, do not be surprised at the painful trial [of persecution] you are suffering . . . But *rejoice* that you participate in the sufferings of Christ, so that you may be overjoyed when His glory is revealed" (1 Pet. 4:12-13).

God-ordained suffering in this world is only the flip-side of God-appointed glory in the world to come. For "suffering is the law of the kingdom" (William C. Burns), and until Jesus returns and establishes peace on this earth, a life totally devoid of suffering will be a life devoid of the fullness of God.

But there is a tremendous amount of suffering that has nothing to do with God's will. Sometimes we suffer because of our sins or because we are ignorant of the promises of God. At other times we suffer because we are not equipped to resist the onslaughts of Satan. But there is a place of suffering *promised* us by the Lord. And that place of suffering is blessed.

No, being sick or depressed is not suffering for Jesus. In fact, it is that kind of suffering Jesus came to relieve! He "went around doing good and healing all who were under the power of the devil, because God was with Him" (Acts 10:38). He revealed the heart of the Father to us by healing all who came to Him in faith. He was the will of God in action. He never refused a one. An unbiased reading of the gospels should settle the question of healing for all time. *The whole man wholly healed has always been God's ideal.*

What about car wrecks, plane crashes and natural disasters — can believers point to these as part of our lot in the Lord? No, these terrible tragedies have nothing to do with suffering for Jesus. They are calamities common to the whole human race. If anything, as children of God, we are promised divine protection from such troubles: "If you make the Most High your dwelling — even the Lord, who is my refuge — then no harm will befall you, no disaster will come near your tent" (Ps. 91:9-10). Dying in an earthquake or wasting away with cancer is *not* part of "carrying the cross." The cross is something we pick up willingly. We can choose to put it down.

But carrying the cross *does* mean following in Jesus' footsteps. And in His footsteps are rejection, brokenheartedness, persecution and death. "There are not two Christ's — an easygoing one for easygoing Christians, and a suffering one for exceptional believers. There is only one Christ" (Hudson Taylor). Are we willing to follow His lead?

We talk about having altar calls, but do we really mean what we say? The altar is the place of sacrifice. The altar is the place of death. We are called to be *living sacrifices,* to live sacrificed lives. There is no other way to please Him. An altar call will cost us our lives.

This is part of our burden: We sacrifice for the Lord. We do without sleep because we must watch and pray. We do without food because we must seek Him with fasting. We do without things because there are others in need. We put others first even when it hurts. All this is suffering for the Lord. We are "not to please ourselves. Each of us should please his neighbor for his good to build him up [this kind of "man-pleasing" is right!]. For even Christ did not please Himself" (Rom. 15:3). And He is our example. Separation, service, sacrifice and suffering — this is the way of the cross.

John Fletcher's wife recounted:
"He was hardly able to relish his dinner if some sick neighbor

had not a part of it; and sometimes, if any one of them was in want, I could not keep the linen in his drawers. . . . Once a poor man, who feared God, being brought into great difficulties, he took down all the pewter from the kitchen shelves, saying, 'This will help you; and I can do without it. A wooden trencher will serve me just as well.'

But "selfish spirits can never understand sacrifice" (Frank Bartleman). Its message seems to cramp their style. If we seek to grab and hold on, to always put our wants first, we will never make Jesus smile. And we will live hollow and empty lives.

Missionaries working in more than seven nations with the organization known as "Christ Is the Answer" live in small tents and trailers so they can be mobile to preach the Word. They travel throughout the countries God has called them to, witnessing by day on the streets and holding evening rallies in their big tent. Some of them are married with children. Their entire family quarters could fit in many of our living rooms. Their bathroom facilities are one-person-at-a-time wooden shacks with large sanitized buckets. They do without the comforts of home — *all for the sake of the lost.* They pour themselves out for the Lord. What else can disciples do? This too is suffering for Him.

And then there is our conflict with the devil. We must remember that we are at war. As *good soldiers* of Messiah Jesus, we are called to *endure hardship* (2 Tim. 2:3) — sometimes at the risk of our lives. One Indonesian believer, newly trained in the principles of spiritual warfare, began preaching several years ago in isolated Muslim villages on the island of Sumatra. For nine months he was rejected, forced to sleep at night in the dangerous jungles. But he knew his Commanding Officer had not called for retreat, so he refused to give up and go home. When his first convert was finally won, a floodgate of souls was opened, and in the next fifteen months over twenty-five thousand were saved. Unshakable determination saw him through.

This man lived as a soldier in combat, and warfare makes heavy demands. "When a nation calls its prime men to battle, homes are broken, weeping sweethearts say their good-byes, businesses are closed, college careers are wrecked, factories are refitted for wartime production, rationing and discomforts are accepted — all for war. Can we do less for the greatest fight that this world has ever known outside of the cross — this end-time siege on sanity, morality, and spirituality?" (Leonard Ravenhill)

We can not afford to let up. Nor can we let our guard down. War requires that we be sober and strong. "Be self-controlled and alert. Your adversary the devil prowls around like a roaring lion looking for someone to devour. Resist him, standing firm in the faith, because you know that your brothers throughout the world are undergoing *the same kind of suffering*" (1 Pet. 5:8-9). We will have some adversity in this life.

But there is a realm of suffering that most of us have never seen. It is the suffering of imprisonment and martyrdom, the suffering of torture and pain. *It is the story of much of the Church.* It is a story being written *today.* From missionaries in Mozambique comes this recent account:

"One of our pastors reported last week that Frelimo government soldiers had forced their way into his church and started shooting at random, killing at least eight people and injuring many. . . . Thousands of innocent civilians are dying at the hands of Frelimo, a large number of them because of their faith in Jesus Christ. A booklet of recent occurrences is being compiled. *The blood of the martyrs is crying out from the ground. We the saints of God must lift our voices in prayer and intercession on behalf of our brothers and sisters. We must be made aware of the truth. How else can we be burdened and moved to pray?* Those in suffering NEED our prayers; they are a source of life and hope. We can bring in the harvest through prayer and bring strength to those in despair" (Rodney and Ella Hein).

"We speak in the name of the persecuted churches. Our brethren slept for years on the concrete of unheated cells, wore prisoner's garb, hungered or ate worse than garbage, were tortured, but loved their tormentors heartily and prayed for their salvation. . . . We ask all to keep before their eyes the martyrs and heroes of the faith" (Richard Wurmbrand).

We are all one Body. "If one part suffers, *every part suffers with it"* (1 Cor. 12:26). "Remember those in prison [for their faith] *as if you were their fellow prisoners,* and those who are mistreated *as if you yourselves were suffering"* (Heb. 13:3). We must keep the suffering Church in our hearts, and do what we can to lighten their load — by praying, by giving, by writing, by caring.

How would you feel if you were violently taken away from your family, put on a starvation diet, brutally beaten, terrorized and harassed — and all the while your *spiritual brothers and sisters,* living in great comfort and ease, didn't even think to pray for you once? How would you feel if you knew that they were interested in stocks and bonds, in the latest news and sports, in game shows and computers, in new church pews and home improvement loans — and they had completely forgotten about you? How would you feel if they sat laughing and feasting with their friends — and you sat completely alone?

On January 19, 1888, missionaries were sent out from Knox Church in Toronto. One young couple was "about to leave for an African field known as 'The White Man's Grave.' The husband said, 'My wife and I have a strange dread in going. We feel much as if were going down into a pit.

We are willing to take the risk and to go if you, our home circle, will promise *to hold the ropes.*' One and all promised.

"Less than two years passed when the wife and the little one God had given them succumbed to the dreaded fever. Soon the husband realized his days too were numbered. Not waiting to send word home of his coming, he started back at once and arrived at the hour of the Wednesday prayer meeting. He slipped in unnoticed, taking a back seat. At the close of the meeting he went forward. An awe came over the people, for death was written on his face. He said:

" 'I am your missionary. My wife and child are buried in Africa and I have come home to die. This evening I listened anxiously, as you prayed, for some mention of your missionary to see if you were keeping your promise, but in vain! You prayed for everything connected with yourselves and your home church, but you forgot your missionary. I see now why I am a failure as a missionary. It is because *you have failed to hold the ropes!*' " (Rosalind Goforth) What an indictment against us!

But Jesus never lets go of the ropes. He cannot be detached from His Body. He is one with His persecuted brothers and He literally feels their pain. When the Lord met Saul on the road to Damascus, He asked him, "Saul, Saul, why do you persecute *Me*? . . . I am Jesus who you are persecuting" (Acts 9:4-5). "The body being hurt, the head in heaven cried out" (Thomas Watson). Shouldn't we cry out as well?

Right now, precious saints of God are suffering untold horrors in "re-education camps" where the authorities try to strip them of their faith. *Some of them have been there for more than two decades.* Others have been put in hospitals for the criminally insane, where they have often been beaten and drugged. *They are totally at the hands of their demented captors.* But Jesus stands with them still. Will we stand with Him — and with them? Or will we be like the disciples in the garden and leave Him — and the suffering Church — alone again? When John Fletcher's wife expressed her concern for his health as she heard him praying for God's people at all hours of the night, he replied, "O Polly, the cause of God lies near my heart!" It must lie near out hearts too.

But the suffering Church is triumphant, as Tertullian said to pagan Rome eighteen centuries ago: *"As often as we are mown down by you, the more we grow in numbers. The blood of Christians is the seed."* In dying, we bear much fruit.

The persecuted saints have been beaten down — but Jesus has lifted them up. They have had to call out to the Lord from the depths. He has reached down and taken them out. They have learned to take refuge in God alone. They have been forced to lean wholly on Him. We should be jealous for the grace they have received. It comes only to those in great need. In our "fullness" we have little room for Him.

The suffering Church stands strong for the faith. Their commitment is measured and sure. They understand that following Jesus could mean death. Although they may lose their families and friends, *they know they love Jesus more.* In their hearts they have counted the cost. There is depth to their "decision" for the Lord.

They live in an environment that is hostile to God — they can not get comfortable there. Some of them have lost all in following Him. Their treasures are not stored up here. *We* may get fooled and become friends with the world, but it is out of the question for them. Convenience is hardly known in their lives — especially in carrying the cross! These saints have probably never seen a microwave oven, and *they have probably never heard our "microwave gospel."* Because their lives are salted with fire, they are an ever-spreading flame.

Benjamin Bedel sold gospel literature in Persia and Mesopotamia for 40 years until his death in 1919. "A linguist, he spoke Syriac, Turkish, Russian, Persian, and Arabic. In Persia alone he sold over thirty thousand copies of Scripture. *Such was his bravery that, when notices were posted up forbidding the sale of Christian Scriptures on pain of death Bedel would stand under the notices, at the main gate of the bazaar, proffering Bibles to any and every one. So did this lone man defy the entrenched might of Islam.* At Nakavand he suffered for his boldness, being beaten on the bare soles of his feet. Under this cruel punishment Bedel three times lost consciousness and each time, as his senses returned, heard the Kutjahids still commanding the servants to beat him until life was gone. 'The same day by God's grace and help I was able to sell eight copies in that bigoted town.' " (Ernest Gordon). There are many such saints around the world today — unknown and unheralded — but putting us all to shame.

In 1948, the two sons of Korean Pastor Son, Tong-In and Tong-Sin, were shot to death by a nineteen year old Marxist during a Communist student uprising. They were killed because they refused to renounce their faith.

"When Pastor Son was brought to identify their bodies, he said only, 'Their shining faces are as lovely as flowers.'

"The uprising was quickly put down and the murderer of the two brothers caught and put on trial. Pastor Son found him with hands tied behind his back, awaiting the death sentence. He hurried to the military authorities. 'Nothing will bring back my boys now, so what is to be gained by killing this one. I am willing to take him and try to make a Christian of him so he could do for God what Tong-In and Tong-Sin left undone.'

"The military officers were momentarily stunned. Finally,

they reluctantly agreed to the proposal and Pastor Son took the murderer of his boys home" (James and Marta Hefley).

This was the perfection of love. It was born out of hardship and pain. The true *deeper life* is not cheap. It must be experienced to be gained.

Jesus "learned obedience through what He suffered" (Heb. 5:8). Will we learn obedience too? The Son was made "perfect through suffering" (Heb. 2:10). There is no other path to follow if we would be perfect in Him. "That is why for Christ's sake, I delight in weaknesses, in insults, in hardships, in persecutions, in difficulties. For when I am weak, then I am strong" (2 Cor. 12:10).

What about us? How strong are we?

Chapter Thirteen

Go Into All The World

In 1865, David Livingstone, the British missionary-explorer, returned to Africa for his third and last time. For almost seven years, this "bearded, toothless, haggard old man" did not see another European. Amidst rumors that he had died, the New York *Herald* sent Henry Stanley to search for him in the jungles of Africa. (It was when Stanley found him that he spoke those famous words, "Dr. Livingstone, I presume.") Stanley had been a worldly reporter who had fought for money on *both* sides of the Civil War. But his time with Livingstone changed him for ever. This was his account:

"For four months and four days I lived with him in the same hut, or the same boat, or the same tent, and I never found a fault in him. I went to Africa as prejudiced against religion as the worst infidel in London. To a reporter like myself, who had only to deal with wars, mass meetings and political gatherings, sentimental matters were quite out of my province. But there came to me a long time for reflection. I was out there away from a worldly world. I saw this solitary old man there, and I asked myself, 'Why does he stop here? What is it that inspires him?' For months after we met I found myself listening to him, wondering at the old man carrying out the words, 'leave all and follow me.' But little by little, seeing his piety, his gentleness, his zeal, his earnestness and how he went quietly about his business, I was converted by him, although he had not tried to do it."

On May 1, 1873, Livingstone was found dead by his servants, kneeling by his cot. As a token of their deep love and respect for him, the natives buried his heart in Africa before carrying his sun-mummified body to the coast — a journey of nine months — where it was returned to England. But Stanley's profound questions still speak to us today: Why did Livingstone stop there, alone in the middle of nowhere? What was it that did inspire him? Why would a man or woman leave friends and family, forsake all earthly comforts, and risk sickness and death among a heathen people? What is it that so many missionaries saw that we do not see today? Why were they so deeply moved while we are so often unmoved?

"My business is to witness for Christ. I make shoes just to pay my expenses" (William Carey). What is our business?

"The longing of my heart would be to go once all round the world before I die, and preach one gospel invitation in the ear of every creature" (William C. Burns). What is the longing of our heart?

"I am sixty-five today . . . *Oh, how I covet, more than a miser does his gold, twenty more years of this soul saving work*" (Jonathan Goforth). What do we covet, more than a miser does his gold?

Consider the example of Adoniram Judson, America's first foreign missionary, born in Massachusetts on August 9, 1788. While preparing for his departure for India and Burma in 1810, he fell in love with Ann (Nancy) Hasseltine. As the prize teenage daughter of a socially prominent family, she was a fun loving young woman before being born again at age fifteen.

After that she was devoted to the Lord. But Judson could not marry her without her father's consent. Listen to the remarkable letter that he wrote to John Hasseltine, himself a relatively new believer:

"I have now to ask, whether you can consent to part with your daughter early next spring, to see her no more in this world; whether you can consent to her departure, and her subjection to the hardships and sufferings of a missionary life; whether you can consent to her exposure to the dangers of the ocean; to the fatal influence of the southern climate of India; to every kind of want and distress; to degradation, insult, persecution, and perhaps a violent death. Can you consent to all this, for the sake of him who left his heavenly home, and died for her and for you; for the sake of perishing, immortal souls; for the sake of Zion, and the glory of God? Can you consent to all this, in hope of soon meeting your daughter in the world of glory, with the crown of righteousness, brightened with the acclamations of praise which shall redound to her Saviour from heathens saved, through her means, from eternal woe and despair?"

Amazingly, her father left the choice to her. Soon she wrote to a friend: "I have about come to the determination to give up all my comforts and enjoyments here, sacrifice my affection to relatives and friends, and go where God, in his providence, shall see fit to place me." In spite of some fears, she knew she could rest in the faithfulness of God, although, as she said, "no female has, to my knowledge, ever left the shores of America to spend her life among the heathen; nor do I yet know, that I shall have a single female companion. But God is my witness, that I have not dared to decline the offer that has been made me, though so many are ready to call it 'a wild and romantic undertaking.' "

The Judson's labored for almost seven years before winning their first convert. After nine years they had baptized only eighteen. Several of their fellow missionaries died. Others left the work. Their first baby was stillborn during their initial voyage from Calcutta to Burma. Their second baby Roger died before reaching his ninth month. Adoniram himself was brutally imprisoned for seventeen months during a crackdown against all foreigners, barely surviving the horribly inhuman treatment. One night, while his raw and bleeding feet were hanging in elevated stocks, swarms of mosquitoes settled on his bare soles, producing excruciating torture.

Then, not long after his release from prison, Adoniram's beloved wife Nancy died. Her constant life of sacrifice and service had finally taken its toll. Just a few weeks later little Maria, their third baby, was suddenly taken from this world. Judson was left utterly alone in a hostile Buddhist land, almost shattered with pain and grief.

Before him lay the prospect of tiger infested jungles, bat infested houses, and a fever infested climate — for life. Behind him lay an almost unimaginable trail of hardship and loss. But he did not leave off from his work. He did not abandon his Bible translating or his preaching and teaching labors. How could he? Eternal souls were at stake. Who else could reach the Burmese as well as he? So he remained for over 20 more years, returning to America only once — and that by necessity, not by choice.

For Judson, missions was a lifetime commitment, and he had no place for those who wanted to come to the missions field on a short-term basis only. "They come out for a few years, with the view of acquiring a stock of credit on which they may vegetate the rest of their days, in the congenial climate of their native land . . . The motto of every missionary, whether preacher, printer, or schoolmaster, ought to be *'Devoted for life.'* "

Adoniram Judson's devotion for life was not in vain. On one occasion, during the great annual festival held at the towering golden Buddhist pagoda in Rangoon, he recorded that he had distributed "nearly ten thousand tracts, giving to none but those who ask . . . Some come two or three months' journey, from the borders of Siam and China — 'Sir, we hear that there is an eternal hell. We are afraid of it. Do give us a writing that will tell us how to escape it.' . . . Others come from the interior of the country, where the name of Jesus Christ is a little known — 'Are you Jesus Christ's man? Give us a writing that tells about Jesus Christ.' " For Judson, it was worth it all. *Today there are more than one million Burmese believers.*

What was it that moved the heart of brilliant young Henry Martyn almost two hundred years ago? He relates that his Cambridge Fellows "thought it a most improper step for me to leave the University to preach to the ignorant heathen, which any person could do." Martyn also found pastoral work difficult, and he had no visible success as a soul-winner. But in spite of all this he had a clear and definite call from God: "May the Lord be pleased to fix this in my mind, that I am in the midst of dying souls, who are thronging to hell. How cruel, how impious to let a brother perish for want of warning."

At one time he would never have sacrificed material well being for the gospel. But now his heart was gripped for India's multitudes. "Ten thousand times more than ever do I feel devoted to that precious work. O gladly shall this base blood be shed, every drop of it, if India can be benefited in one of these children, if but one of these base creatures of God Almighty might be brought home to this duty."

Saying good-bye to his homeland was heartbreaking for him. It was even more difficult to leave behind Lydia Grenfell, a young woman whom he passionately loved and would have married, if not for his fear that marriage could be a hindrance to his call. To add to all the difficulties, his own frail health was failing. "Oh my dear friends in England," he recorded in his diary, "when we spoke with exultation of the mission to the heathen, whilst in the midst of health and joy and hope, what an imperfect idea did we form of the sufferings by which it must be accomplished." Yet he gave himself without reserve, always putting the needs of others first. His efforts in India and Persia were Herculean, and his saintliness and godliness legendary.

Why did he give himself so unsparingly to the work of the Lord, often standing alone against "British indifference, Indian apathy, and Muslim hostility"? Why did he refuse to let up or back down, even when his own body was rapidly deteriorating? "The man who slaved away his life among the people whom the lowest clerk of the East India Company would have despised, and who dragged his dying body over many hundreds of miles of sea and mountains, did it for this purpose: to do the will of God, and to save men and women from destruction" (R. T. France).

And what was it that constrained Scottish-born John Paton to go as a pioneer missionary to the "cannibals" of the South Sea Islands, devoting almost five decades to the work? While struggling through university, divinity and medical studies in Scotland, Paton had been sustained "by the lofty aim which," he said, "burned all these years bright within my soul, namely to be owned and used by Him for the salvation of perishing men."

He became grieved when no one in his church synod responded to the need for a new missionary to be sent to the South Seas. "The Lord kept saying within me, 'Since none better-qualified can be got, rise and offer yourself.' Almost overpowering was the impulse to answer aloud, 'Here I am, send me.'"

But Paton did not want to mistake his own emotions for the call of God, so he continued in prayer and careful deliberation for a few more days "to look at the proposal from every angle . . . I felt a growing assurance that this was the call of God to His servant. The wail and claims of the heathen were constantly sounding in my ears. I saw them perishing for lack of the knowledge of the true God and His Son Jesus, while my Green Street people [in Scotland] had the open Bible and all the means of grace within easy reach."

Yet his decision to go was opposed by almost everybody. "Some retorted upon me, 'There are heathen at home; let us seek and save, first of all, the lost ones perishing at our doors.' " We must evangelize our home front first, before we worry about the rest of the world. Aren't their millions of sinners living all around us? Isn't it logical and right to preach to them first?

Paton agreed that, in fact, there were many heathen at home. "This I felt to be most true, and an appalling fact; but I unfailingly observed that those who made this retort neglected those home heathen themselves . . . [Let's listen carefully. This message is for us!] They would ungrudgingly spend more on a fashionable party at dinner or tea, on concert or ball or theatre, or on some ostentatious display, or worldly or selfish indulgence, ten times more, perhaps in a single day, than they would give in a year, or in half a lifetime, for the conversion of the whole heathen world, either at home or abroad." How powerful, and yet, how pathetically true!

In 1906, at the age of eighty-two and just months after losing his wife of forty-one years, he was traveling to speak at a meeting in Australia when he was thrown from his buggy and knocked unconscious. But he insisted on preaching, bandaged head and all. "What have I been spared for," he said, "if it is not to use every remaining opportunity to plead for the perishing heathen." And what have we been spared for, if not to respond to Paton's plea, to respond to the cries of the lost, to respond to the call of the Lord. *Why else are we here?*

There are more lost people alive today than ever before in history. And we have less time than ever to reach them. How can we sit back? Doesn't it trouble us that there are *one billion* souls who have never heard the name of Jesus? Doesn't this move us to action?

There are more than *12,000* distinct people groups without a native church. Out of the 6100 languages spoken today, *over half* of them do not have even 1 verse of the Bible, and not even *one tenth* of them have a complete New Testament. Earth's population grows by over a *quarter of a million* human beings every day. Jesus bled for each of them. What in the world are we waiting for?

At this very moment, all over the world, there are missionaries and native workers who could reach a hundred times more people if they only had adequate funding. Yet we live here like kings and princes, getting fatter and fuller each day. Can't we see the folly of this in light of the harvest? Can't we see that something in our mind set is wrong? Can we still turn a deaf ear to the needs of our brothers? Can we refuse to sacrificially give?

On every inhabited continent, there are multitudes of perishing souls. God knows each one of them by name. To this day, they are living in ignorance and darkness. They are imprisoned by the devil and locked up in their sins. But we have the Key that will set them free. We have the eternal Answer for their lives. We have the Truth and the Light. Are there any of us who will arise and go? Are there any of us who will leave all — *it is only for this short life* — in view of the glories to come?

We must give serious thought to our ways. We have lost sight of a fundamental truth. Jesus gave His life for this dying world. Can we give any less? Missions is the very heart of the gospel. *Being saved means being sent.* The nations are perishing without hope. Our time is running out. We must reach these precious people before it is too late. *If we don't give or go, who will?*

This is the Word of the Lord:
"Consider and give ear: Forget your people and your father's house . . . *Go* into all the world and preach the good news to all creation . . . *Go* and make disciples of all nations . . . As the Father has sent Me, I am sending you . . . *Go!* I am sending you."

Chapter Fourteen

Redeeming The Time

Early in 1832, nineteen-year-old Robert Murray M'Cheyne, just beginning his preparation for the ministry, entered these words in his diary: "Feb. 2 — Not a trait worth remembering! And yet these four-and-twenty hours must be accounted for." Will this be the verdict at the end of our days? "Not a trait worth remembering" — yet we must give account!

We are often more concerned with the quantity of life than with the quality of life. We want to be healthy, active and strong, living our lives to the full. But we can live ninety years and still have an empty life. We can span a whole century and waste it all away. One diamond is of greater worth than a thousand ordinary stones.

"How shall I feel at the judgment, if multitudes of missed opportunities pass before me in full review, and all my excuses prove to be disguises of my cowardice and pride?" (W. E. Sangster) How will we answer to God on that Day?

But our problem isn't only cowardice and pride. Some of us are sleepwalking our way through life! How will we feel at the judgment if multitudes of missed opportunities pass before us in full review — and we find ourselves totally unaware that we ever had them? What an awful moment it will be for many of us when we see that life has completely passed us by — and it is too late to do anything about it!

Jonathan Edwards made 70 resolutions by which he patterned his life. Here are just a few of them: "*Resolved,* Never to lose one moment of time, but to improve it in the most profitable way I possibly can. . . . *Resolved,* To live with all my might while I do live. . . . *Resolved,* Never to do anything which I should be afraid to do, if it were the last hour of my life." It was Jonathan Edwards who prayed, "Lord, stamp eternity on my eyes." He lived every day in view of forever. "There is nothing like the light of eternity to show what is real and what is not" (Catherine Booth).

Many of us let the circumstances of the moment rule us. We are governed by the pressing needs of the hour. We do not know how to make our schedules submit. We are too busy to accomplish anything of value for God. What matters the least occupies most of our time. What matters the most seldom gets done. Our life is a series of unfulfilled goals. There is plenty of action, but little lasting satisfaction. Our lives are running us instead of us — under God — running our lives.

We must ask ourselves some pointed questions: Are the things we are living for worth Messiah dying for? Are we making the most of every opportunity? Are we living to bring glory to God? Do we realize that we are only passing through this world? "Beware the barrenness of a busy life" (Corrie Ten-Boom).

The few short years we have on this planet could be marked by frustration and futility, or they could be marked by fruitfulness and fulfillment. Who knows just how much could be accomplished through one life yielded up to God? Who knows what God could do through you, if you yielded your all to

Him? "Consider what you are missing, both for time and eternity, if you love Jesus with only half a heart" (Basilea Schlink).

William Carey began his career as an uneducated shoemaker in England. He ended his life in India as the father of modern missions, serving also as Professor of Oriental Languages at Fort William College in Calcutta. And he was almost entirely self-taught! Who would have ever dreamed of such a thing? To Carey it was no surprise. This was his motto for life: "Expect great things from God. Attempt great things for God." Yes — "All things are possible for him who believes" (Mark 9:23).

While earning honors at Cambridge in mathematics and classics, Henry Martyn was known as "the man who never lost an hour." He continued in this pattern as a believer and missionary. When he died at the tender age of thirty-one, after six short years of missionary labor, he had made excellent translations of the entire New Testament into Hindustani (Urdu) and Persian, in addition to translating the Psalms into Persian and the Book of Common Prayer into Hindustani. The work of several decades was accomplished in less than 70 months.

Just think of what we could do in many years of service — if we maintained a steady pace for God and continued to fuel the fires of our heart. "Never be lacking in zeal, but keep your spiritual fervor . . . and fan into flame the gift of God which is in you . . . for at the proper time we will reap a harvest if we do not give up" (Rom. 12:11; 2 Tim. 1:6; Gal. 6:9).

We don't necessarily have to suffer what some of these men and women did — to waste away and die of tuberculosis in a foreign land, to experience deprivation and malnutrition, to run ourselves into the grave — in order to accomplish the work of the Lord. But we should be stirred to action by their total devotion to God.

David Brown, a friend and fellow-worker of Henry Martyn wrote to him saying, "you burn with the intenseness and rapid blaze of heated phosphorous." This was the fulfillment of the desire which Martyn inscribed in his diary when he first arrived in India: "Now let me burn out for God."

George Whitefield also burned red-hot for the Lord. From the ages of twenty to fifty-six, he delivered about 30,000 sermons, often preaching *40 to 60 hours a week*. He preached to crowds of up to 40,000 — without amplification and with hardly any advertising. During his 34 years of ministry, he preached in virtually every town in England, Scotland and Wales, visiting Ireland as well. He sailed the Atlantic seven times, and won thousands of souls to the Lord in both northern and southern America — all the while using eighteenth-century means of transportation.

"Who . . . would think it possible that a person a little above the age of manhood could speak in a single week and that for years — in general forty hours, and in very many weeks, sixty — and that to thousands; and after this labour, instead of taking any rest, should be offering up prayers and intercessions, with hymns and spiritual songs, as his manner was, in every house to which he was invited? The truth is, that in point of labour this extraordinary servant of God did as much in a few weeks as most of those who exert themselves are able to do in the space of a year" (Henry Venn).

How did Whitefield accomplish so much in so short a period of time? (Let's not forget that he also built and maintained a large orphanage in Georgia, and he carried out a massive correspondence with people in almost every corner of the world.) It is true that he had an overwhelming burden for souls.

He used to pray, "Lord, give me souls or take my soul!" But he also knew how to redeem the time for the Lord. Each night he would judge his actions for the day, using a carefully thought out list of fifteen criteria:

"Have I,

1. Been fervent in private prayer?
2. Used stated hours of prayer?
3. Used [spontaneous vocal prayer] each hour?
4. After or before every deliberate conversation or action, considered how it might tend to God's glory?
5. After each pleasure, immediately given thanks?
6. Planned business for the day?
7. Been simple and [self-controlled] in everything?
8. Been zealous in undertaking and active in doing what good I could?
9. Been meek, cheerful, affable in everything I said or did?
10. Been proud, vain, unchaste, or enviable of others?
11. [Been self-controlled] in eating and drinking? Thankful? Temperate in sleep?
12. Taken time for giving thanks according to [William] Law's rules?
13. Been diligent in studies?
14. Thought or spoken unkindly of anyone?
15. Confessed all sins?"

Is it any wonder that he was a leading figure in the great eighteenth-century revival in England and America?

But Whitefield did not sit idly on his laurels. At one point he noted: "My constant work now is, preaching about fifteen times a week. . . . And *my greatest grief is that I can do no more for Him who hath done and suffered so much for me.*"

In 1753, at the age of thirty-nine, he wrote, "Let none of my friends cry to such a sluggish, lukewarm, unprofitable worm,

Spare thyself. Rather spur me on, I pray you, with an Awake, thou sleeper, and begin to do something for thy God." And in 1754, having recovered from some serious illnesses, he wrote to Charles Wesley from America, "My health is wonderful . . . though I ride whole nights, and have been frequently exposed to great thunders, violent lightnings and heavy rains, yet I am rather better than usual, and as far as I can judge am not yet to die. O that I might at length begin to live. I am ashamed of my sloth and lukewarmness, and long to be on the stretch for God."

When Whitefield was urged to slow down and take better care of himself, he replied "It is better to wear out than to rust out." To this day his ministry still shines.

It was from John Wesley, Whitefield's contemporary, that he learned the importance of a disciplined and regimented lifestyle. This was Wesley's Rule of Conduct:
Do all the good you can,
By all the means you can,
In all the ways you can,
In all the places you can,
At all the times you can,
To all the people you can,
As long as ever you can.

In Wesley's 53 years of ministry (he died at the age of 88), he raised up and organized a radical army of lay preachers, travelled about 5,000 miles a year by horseback or carriage, preached over 50,000 sermons, wrote 233 books and pamphlets (ranging from biblical commentaries to medical treatises), as well as read and reviewed everything of interest that was published in Europe. He pushed his five foot four inch, one hundred-twenty-pound frame to the limit, and stored up for himself an eternal treasure that will never fade or perish.

In 1771, John Fletcher described Wesley as flying "with unwearied diligence through the three kingdoms, calling sinners to repentance and to the healing fountain of Jesus' blood. Though oppressed with the weight of near seventy years, and the cares of nearly 30,000 souls, he shames still, by his unabated zeal and immense labors, all the young ministers in England, perhaps in Christendom. He has generously blown the gospel trumpet, and rode twenty miles, before most of the professors who despise his labours, have left their downy pillows. As he begins the day, the week, the year, so he concludes them, still intent upon extensive services for the glory of the Redeemer and the good of souls."

It was John Wesley who said, "Though I am in haste, I am never in a hurry." May his example challenge us today.

***

On December 18, 1831, after spending an evening too lightly, Robert Murray M'Cheyne wrote in his diary: "My heart must break off from all these things. What right have I to steal and abuse my Master's time? 'Redeem it,' He is crying to me."

What is He crying to us?

Chapter Fifteen

The Rude Awakening

Two hundred and fifty years ago a tremendous revival swept our land. Church attendance increased radically, while immorality and drunkenness decreased dramatically. Many thousands of believers came alive and multitudes of unsaved were truly born again. At that time George Whitefield said: "I love those that thunder out the word! The Christian world is in a deep sleep. Nothing but a loud voice can waken them out of it!" This was the Great Awakening.

But today the Church of America does not need a Great Awakening. *We need a Rude Awakening.* A spirit of slumber is over the Body *and we are under a great deception.* We think we are in a last days revival, but we are really in a fight for survival. We think we are ready to take the whole world, but it is the world that has taken us.

It is now or never for the people of God. Either we dream on or we face the facts. But one way or another, we will be aroused from our stupor — by an internal stirring or by an external shaking; by inward perseverance or by outward persecution; by judging ourselves or by being judged. Either way, our peaceful sleep is about to come to an abrupt end.

Take a good, hard look at our spiritual state.

Our country has a population of 250 million people, and we have well over 350 thousand Protestant clergy — *1 for every 700 Americans.* Yet for the 5.25 billion human beings outside of our land, we have less than 50 thousand full-time Protestant missionaries on the field — *1 for every 115 thousand souls!* For every *1,000* American evangelicals, we send out *less than 1* missionary — including short-term workers. Not even *one tenth of one percent* of the American "born again church" is presently sharing the gospel in a foreign land. New Zealand and Norway send out far more missionaries per capita than we do. We are not as great as we think. *We need a Rude Awakening.*

"Evangelicals in the United States earn $700 billion per year. Of this, they give $21 billion, or 3.0 percent to the Church. Of that [21 billion], $2.1 billion, or 0.3 percent goes to missions; and of that, $20 million, or 0.0029 percent, goes to unreached peoples. . . . How much more could the Christians of the world give if we really gave sacrificially? How much more would we give if we really believed that a million people were going into eternity each week without Jesus Christ?" (Nate Krupp) Would it be more than one-third of a penny per dollar? *We need a Rude Awakening.*

We know of the spiritual darkness in Iran: Fanatical Muslims rule the land and no missionaries are welcome there. We have heard of the terrible persecutions that have taken place in Vietnam: Many pastors have given their lives and many others have spent long years in prison. Yet the evangelical churches in Iran and Vietnam are growing at a faster percentage than the evangelical church in America! *We need a Rude Awakening.*

We sometimes pray for those who have endured hardship for the gospel behind the Iron and Bamboo Curtains. But believers there have often prayed for *us* — that God would shake us up (even with persecution!), that we would die to our worldliness and selfishness, that we would learn the meaning of sacrifice, and that we would truly sell out for the Lord. While we see all our luxuries as great heavenly blessings, they see them as excess earthly baggage that is always pulling us down. The suffering Church is concerned about us! *We need a Rude Awakening.*

The United States is now considered a ripe mission field. There are presently over six thousand foreign missionaries in our midst that have been sent *to* America to reach *us!* And they are not just witnessing to people of their own nationality — they see how lost many of us are. There are plenty of "native heathen" in our land — we have dozens of unreached people groups here too. They are dying without God in our own back yard! *We need a Rude Awakening.*

We are at home in a fallen world. Many of us have gone years without leading any of our friends or neighbors to the Lord. Yet God "has committed to *us* the ministry of reconciliation" (2 Cor. 5:19). We have fallen miserably short! We work side by side by with people who are perishing. But we are too much like them to change them. What would we be changing them to? If some of us confronted them with their sins, we would end up condemning ourselves! *We need a Rude Awakening.*

Family life has greatly degenerated. We are lazy when it comes to the home. There is so little discipline enforced, so little respect produced. Compromise is almost our Christian philosophy: do it the world's way, only not quite as bad! Give in to peer pressure, and don't seem extreme! Our values are made of rubber, not steel. They have not been forged on the anvil of godly conviction. They are as changeable as the newest fashions and fads. Our children are allowed too much liberty. They set so many of their own standards — what they watch, what they wear, how they look. But "a child who gets his own way brings shame to his mother" (Prov. 29:15, NASB), and judgment fell upon Eli's "family forever because of the sin he knew about; *his sons made themselves contemptible, and he failed to restrain them"* (1 Sam. 3:13). We have fallen short here too —we have not kept our children on course! We often treat them as burdens instead of blessings, as if they were always getting in the way of *our* lives. We have been brain washed by society after all. We have not taken a stand for the home. Losing here, we lose all. *We need a Rude Awakening.*

We have become completely accustomed to sin. The mayor of our nation's capitol was *video taped in the act* of purchasing and smoking crack. He admitted to being an alcoholic. A married man, his unfaithfulness was hardly hidden. Yet he continued to serve out his mayoral term! He has been hailed as a *hero* and a *victim* by other black mayors in our land! Where is our moral outrage? Where is our revulsion to corruption? Where is our public outcry? *We need a Rude Awakening.*

It is true that our liberal media distorts the real state of our nation. They portray pro-abortionists and gays as the progressive majority while believers are presented as the regressive minority. You would think that we were hopelessly outnumbered. Yet many Americans — maybe even most Americans — claim to be pro-life, pro-family, pro-morality. But is this really good news? Our own words testify against us! If *we* have stopped watching violent, lewd and anti-God television (remember, we boast of large numbers!), why are the ratings still so high? If *we* who are so many no longer buy off-color magazines and tabloids, why are new ones being published every year? *If our children* don't listen to punk rock and heavy metal groups, whose children *are* buying their records by the millions? We talk the right talk but walk the wrong walk. Our hatred of sin is paper thin. We have more cliches than convictions. Radical feminists are more militant than we are! *We need a Rude Awakening.*

We have heard of the coming apostasy. Lawlessness will increase and the love of many will grow cold (Matt. 24:12). We are sure it will happen — *in the future.* But our vision is sadly blurred. The apostasy has already begun! Lawlessness has reached epidemic proportions — our society is saturated with sin. Evil has never been more available. It is so easy for us to stray: a flick of the switch brings pornography into our homes; a simple phone call imports perversion. Seductive spirits are overtaking our land. And there is a plague of *mindlessness* too. We waste away priceless hours that can never be retrieved — sharpening our video game skills. Our high-tech computers do our thinking for us, and we worship transfixed at their screens. We are a backsliding body, and we know it not! We are falling away, and we are unaware! Corruption has infiltrated our ranks. Godly examples are rare. So few are truly passionate for the Lord. His fire burns low in our hearts. Iniquity abounds, holiness is scarce. The love of many has already grown cold! *We need a Rude Awakening.*

"Nothing is more to be feared than too long a peace. You are deceived if you think that a Christian can live without persecution. He suffers the greatest persecution of all who lives under none. A storm puts a man on his guard and obliges him to exert his utmost efforts to avoid shipwreck" (Jerome). But we have relaxed in the calm. We have enjoyed "too long a peace." We have thought it was because we had triumphed, as if Satan were put under our feet. Actually things are different. We have fallen asleep in his lap! *We need a Rude Awakening.*

BUT WAIT!

Don't give up now! Don't throw up your hands in despair! There is a reason that we must wake up: THE MORNING IS

DRAWING NEAR. The time for sleeping is over! A great light is ready to dawn. The darkness will soon disappear. *Oh, be stirred and get out of your bed!*

"*The hour has come for you to wake up from your slumber,* because our salvation is nearer now than when we first believed. *The night is nearly over; the day is almost here.* So let us put aside the deeds of darkness and put on the armor of light. Let us behave decently, *as in the daytime,* not in orgies and drunkenness, not in sexual immorality and debauchery, not in dissension and jealousy. Rather, *clothe yourselves* with the Lord Jesus Christ, and do not think about how to gratify the desires of the sinful nature" (Rom. 13:11-14). We must not be found naked when He comes!

"*You are all sons of the light and sons of the day.* We do not belong to the night or to the darkness. So then, *let us not be like others who are asleep,* but let us be alert and self-controlled. For those who sleep, sleep at night, and those who get drunk, get drunk at night. *But since we belong to the day,* let us be self-controlled, putting on faith as a breastplate, and the hope of salvation as a helmet" (1 Thes. 5:5-8). Let us live as children of the light!

"This is why it is said, 'Wake up, O sleeper, rise from the dead, and Christ will shine on you" (Eph. 5:14). God is speaking, God is urging, "AWAKE!"

Daybreak is fast approaching. The darkness will soon be past. The final outpouring draws nearer. The season of harvest is here. Consider the signs of the times. Wipe slumber away from your eyes.

> We were born for a day such as this.
> It is time for the triumph of God.

Chapter Sixteen

The Times Of Refreshing Must Come!

Peter was an eye-witness of the glory of the Lord. He saw Jesus heal the sick and raise the dead. He saw Him drive out demons and feed the hungry. He saw Him as He suffered and he saw Him when He rose. He saw Him ascend to heaven.

Then, on the day of Pentecost, Peter *experienced* the glory — he was immersed in the Spirit on fire. His own being became super-charged with God. He preached with authority and thousands were saved. He spoke with power and cripples danced for joy. He was soaked with a deluge from on high.

But Peter didn't stop there. In fact, he said there was more. There was a promise from God to the people: *the times of refreshing must come!* "Repent, then, and turn to God, so that your sins may be wiped out, that times of refreshing may come from the [presence of the] Lord, and that He may send the Messiah, who has been appointed for you — even Jesus. He must remain in heaven until the time comes for God to restore everything, as He promised long ago through His holy prophets" (Acts 3:19-21).

Repentance . . . refreshing . . . return . . . restoration: this is the program of God. *Repentance* unlocks the door, and then the *refreshing* comes. And *after* the *refreshing*, the Lord will *return*. And *then* He will fully *restore*. Until then, "He must remain in heaven." First the *showers*, then the *Son*; first the *rain*, then the *return*; first the *outpouring*, then the *appearing*. We will be drenched before He descends. Even now, there are rain clouds in sight . . .

All over the world, God's Spirit is on the move. "There were fewer than 10 million Christians in Africa in 1900, but the projection for 2000 is 324 million." In Latin America, "evangelical Christianity grew from a mere 50,000 in 1900 to a projected 137 million in 2000. . . . In the early 1980's it was estimated that over 20,000 Chinese were being converted to Christianity every day" (Peter Wagner). Even in the extremist Hindu kingdom of Nepal, shrouded by the Himalayan mountains, the Lord has found for Himself a people: in 1960, there were only 25 baptized believers. By 1989, there were over 50,000 — in spite of years of intense government opposition. And this is only the beginning.

On October 22, 1905, a visitation began in Dohnavur, India, among the girls being ministered to by Amy Carmichael, girls who were once temple prostitutes. "At the close of a morning service, [Amy] was obliged to stop, overwhelmed with the sudden realization of the inner force of things. It was impossible even to pray."

This was her description:
    "It was so startling and dreadful — I can use no other word — that details escape me. Soon the whole upper half of the church was on its face on the floor, crying to God, each boy and girl, man and woman oblivious of all others. The sound was like the sound of the waves or strong wind in the

trees. . . . The hurricane of prayer continued for over four hours. 'They passed like four minutes;' for the next two weeks they gave themselves to the Word and prayer; counseling around the clock, almost the whole compound got saved; it deeply affected the village" (Winkie Pratney). As one of the little girls said, "Jesus came to Dohnavur."

But Jesus did not come only to Dohnavur. He came all over the world. From Wales to Indonesia, from Korea to Azusa Street, His Spirit was being poured out. The beginning of the twentieth century saw the greatest spontaneous worldwide moving of God in history. It was as if dozens of unrelated brush fires broke out at once. The flames were leaping in many countries! *Yet there is much more that could come in our day.* The final blaze will scorch every nation. Not one will be left unsinged.

God is only looking for yielded vessels, vessels that are suited for Him. They must be emptied of selfish ambition and dead to human agendas, dedicated wholly to the purposes of heaven. They must be men and women who will not count their lives dear, who will give themselves freely for this world. God is calling for workers who will pay any price and make any sacrifice — as long as it is for the glory of the Lord. He is searching for laborers who will go anywhere and do anything — if only souls can be saved. There is really no telling what God will do — if we will respond to His call. Just look at what He has accomplished through *ordinary human beings* who have obeyed His voice in faith.

John G. Lake had just returned to his home in Spokane one day when he received an urgent call. His secretary, Mrs. Graham, was dying.

"Immediately I hurried to the place. One of my ministers' wives met me at the door and said, 'You are too late; she is gone.'

"As I stepped inside, the minister was coming out of the room. He said, 'She has not breathed for a long time.'

"But looking on that woman, I thought of how God Almighty had raised her out of death three years before; *how He had miraculously given her back her womb, ovaries, and tubes which had been removed in operations; how she had married and conceived a child.* [After having all her reproductive organs removed, God had totally restored them in answer to Lake's prayer.]

"As these thoughts arose, my heart flamed!

"I took that woman up off the pillow and called on God for the lightnings of heaven to blast the power of death and deliver her. I commanded her to come back and stay. She came back after having not breathed for 23 minutes!" This is the power of God.

In 1985, a Kenyan born American evangelist of Indian descent was preaching in Pakistan. It had been his spiritual discipline to spend 40 days in fasting and prayer *twice* every year. Now he was reaping the fruit. As he declared the gospel to the crowds, he noticed a poor old woman sitting on the ground. His heart went out to her when he saw her. She was totally blind from birth, her eyes just sunken sockets. But suddenly the Spirit moved — and when He moves *everything* is possible. In a moment's time this woman was ecstatic with joy. While the message was being preached, *God gave her two new eyes* — and no one had even prayed for her. For the first time in her life she could see. Jesus had honored His Word. He still lives to save and to heal. And He wants to do much, much more — if we will only clear out the way.

Times of refreshing are coming, times that will quench our deepest spiritual thirst and fulfill the dreams we have had in

God. The *LORD* will perform signs and wonders. *Multitudes* will be genuinely saved. Orthodox Jews will call on Yeshua; Muslims will be converted in droves. Atheists will bow down in awe; agnostics will cry "He is Lord!" There will be no way to record all the miracles. The Spirit will cover the earth. *But we must get rid of the sin* — and then the tidal wave will come. Uncleanness is a dam to God's flood.

Remember the apostle's words:

"Repent, then, and turn to God." Things happen when we truly turn back! Repentance brings life, not death. It gets us on track and points us towards God. It renews us and starts us afresh.

". . . so that your sins may be wiped out" and removed from the record for good. There is no need to be blemished any longer. What attractiveness can our sins possibly hold? God is ready to blot them all out, to wipe them completely away. Will you yield yourself wholly to God, and begin a new era in Him?

". . . that times of refreshing may come from the Lord." It is certain, it is sure, they will come! The Lord has not spoken in vain. His promises are tested and true. He has never broken a one. He will not disappoint us or fail. He is faithful, forever, for sure. His reality obliterates doubt. He is God in Word and in deed. He can do *anything* through *anyone* who will give *everything* to Him.

Can He call on you?

References

I would like to thank Frank Kaleb Jansen of the U.S. Center for World Missions in Pasadena, California, for discussing many of the missions and world statistics which are quoted throughout this book, especially in chapters thirteen and fifteen. For further information, see *Target Earth*, ed. Frank Kaleb Jansen (Global Mapping International/University of the Nations, 1989).

Page 4 — Richard Wurmbrand, "The Voice of the Martyrs," December, 1989, p. 3. ("The Voice of the Martyrs" is the monthly newsletter of Christian Missions to the Communist World, Inc.)

Page 4 — Johanna Veenstra, quoted by Ruth A. Tucker, *From Jerusalem to Irian Jaya* (Zondervan, 1983), p. 247.

Page 5 — Johannes Schneider, *Theological Dictionary of the New Testament*, Vol. VII, ed. Gerhard Friedrich, Eng. tr. Geoffrey W. Bromiley (Eerdmans, 1971), pp. 573-574.

Page 9 — A. W. Tozer, *Keys to the Deeper Life* (rev. ed., Creation House, 1984), p. 76 (originally published in *The Tozer Pulpit*, Vol. 6 [Christian Publications, 1975], pp. 56-57).

Page 10 — For information on Francis Asbury, see *Christian History*, Vol. VIII, No. 3, Issue 23, pp. 22-23, and Charles Ludwig, *Francis Asbury: God's Circuit Rider* (Mott Media, 1984), p. xii.

Pages 16-17 — A. W. Tozer, *The Best of A. W. Tozer* (Baker, 1978), p. 101 (originally from the book, *That Incredible Christian*).

Pages 17-18 — J. Edwin Orr, *My All, His All* (International Awakening Press, 1989), p. 7.

Pages 21-22 — John Pollock, *George Whitefield and the Great Awakening* (Lion Publishing, 1972), pp. 229-230; see also Arnold Dallimore, *George Whitefield*, Vol. II (Banner of Truth, 1980), p. 388.

Page 23 — Catherine Booth, *The Writings of Catherine Booth, Aggressive Christianity* (The Salvation Army, 1986), p. 11.

Pages 23-24 — George Whitefield, *Select Sermons of George Whitefield*, ed. J. C. Ryle, (repr. Banner of Truth, 1985), p. 79.

Pages 24-25 — Charles Finney, *Lectures on Revivals of Religion* (Revell, N.D.), pp. 387 and 231-232.

Page 25 — Charles Wesley, quoted by Arnold Dallimore, *A Heart Set Free* (Crossway, 1988), p. 84, my italics.

Page 25 — Hudson Taylor, quoted from his autobiography, *Hudson Taylor* (Bethany, N.D.), p. 14.

Pages 25-26 — John Hyde, quoted from *Praying Hyde*, ed. Captain E. G. Carré (Bridge Publishing, 1982), p. 116.

Page 26 — Jonathan Goforth, quoted from Rosalind Goforth, *Jonathan Goforth* (Bethany, 1986), p. 21.

Page 26 — William C. Burns, quoted from R. Strang Miller in *Five Pioneer Missionaries* (Banner of Truth, 1965), pp. 98 and 128.

Pages 26-27 — John G. Lake, quoted from *The John G. Lake Sermons on Dominion Over Demons, Disease and Death*, ed. Gordon Lindsay (repr. Christ for the Nations, 1982), p. 86; *The New John G. Lake Sermons*, ed. Gordon Lindsay (repr. Christ for the Nations, 1981), pp. 27-28.

Page 27 — Evan Roberts, quoted from Elfion Evans, *The Welsh Revival of 1904* (Evangelical Press of Wales, 1969), p. 70, my italics.

Page 33 — Winkie Pratney, *Revival* (Whitaker, 1983), p. 26.

Page 34 — Catherine Booth, *Aggressive Christianity*, p. 17.

Pages 41-42 — Smith Wigglesworth, *Ever Increasing Faith* (rev. ed., Gospel Publishing House, 1971), p. 99.

Page 44 — The account of the talented young fund raiser was shared with me by a high level executive in "Christian marketing."

Pages 44-45 — Johann Teztel, quoted in J. H. Merle D'Aubigné, *History of the Reformation of the Sixteenth Century* (repr., Baker, 1987), pp. 86-87.

Page 49 — George Mueller, quoted in Roger Steer, *Delighted in God*, (rev. ed., Harold Shaw, 1981), p. 40. The financial statistics regarding Mueller's ministry were compiled by my graduate student Pastor Jamie Cowen, who consulted the Library of Congress for the equivalent amounts in today's dollars.

Page 52 — The pornography statistics quoted by the *Christ for the Nations* magazine, Feb. 1990, p. 7, were adapted from the Plymouth Rock Foundation Fac-Sheet.

Page 54 — The Saudi Arabian crime statistics were supplied to me by the Saudi Arabian Embassy in Washington, D.C.

Page 57 — The Scriptures cited are Heb. 12:25, 2:2, 10:31.

Page 62 — A. W. Tozer, *The Best of A. W. Tozer,* p. 179 (originally from the book, *Man: The Dwelling Place of God*).

Page 70 — Thomas Watson, *The Doctrine of Repentance* (repr. Banner of Truth, 1987), p. 32.

Page 70 — George Whitefield, quoted by Arnold Dallimore, *George Whitefield*, Vol. I, (Banner of Truth, 1970) p. 6.

Page 72 — George Whitefield, quoted from John Pollock, *Great Awakening*, p. 239; Dallimore, *Whitefield*, Vol. I, p. 6; and Pollock, p. 239.

Pages 73-74 — Catherine Booth, *The Writings of Catherine Booth, Godliness* (The Salvation Army, 1986), p. 110.

Page 75 — Mrs. Polly Fletcher, quoted by John Wesley in Frank Whaling, ed., *John and Charles Wesley. Selected Writings and Hymns* (Paulist Press, 1981), pp. 155-156.

Pages 77-78 — Richard Wurmbrand, "The Voice of the Martyrs," December, 1989, p. 4.

Page 78 — John G. Lake, *Dominion*, pp. 54 and 53.

Pages 81-82 — Smith Wigglesworth, *Ever Increasing Faith*, pp. 147-148; 142, 146, 148; 151.

Pages 82-83 — John G. Lake, *Spiritual Hunger and Other Sermons*, ed. Gordon Lindsay (repr. Christ for the Nations, 1987), pp. 75 and 69.

Page 83 — Uggo Bassi's quote was shared with me by Leonard and Martha Ravenhill.

Page 83 — Evan Phillips, quoted in Elfion Evans, *The Welsh Revival of 1904*, p. 72.

Page 86 — William C. Burns, quoted from Strang Miller, *Five Pioneer Missionaries*, p. 113.

Pages 87-88 — Mrs. John Fletcher, *John and Charles Wesley*, p. 152.

Page 88 — Frank Bartleman, *Another Wave of Revival* (Whitaker, 1982), p. 28.

Pages 88-89 — The account of the Indonesian believer was reported firsthand to Ralph Mahoney, president of World M.A.P.

Page 89 — Leonard Ravenhill, *Revival God's Way* (Bethany, 1983), p. 127.

Pages 89-90 — Rodney and Ella Hein, from their letter printed in the January, 1990 issue of the Christ for the Nations "World Prayer and Share Letter," p. 3, my italics.

Page 90 — Richard Wurmbrand, "The Voice of the Martyrs," April, 1990, p. 3.

Pages 90-91 — Rosalind Goforth, *Jonathan Goforth*, pp. 36-37.

Page 91 — Thomas Watson, *Repentance*, p. 11.

Page 92 — Mrs. John Fletcher, *John and Charles Wesley*, p. 155.

Page 92 — Tertullian, *Apologeticus*, 50, 13.

Page 93 — For Benjamin Bedel see Ernest Gordon, *A Book of Protestant Saints* (repr. Prarie Press, 1968), pp. 363-364.

Page 93-94 — For Pastor Son see James and Marta Hefley, *By Their Blood. Christian Martyrs of the 20th Century* (Baker, 1979), pp. 97-98

Pages 94-95 — For David Livingstone, see Ruth Tucker, *From Jerusalem*, p 153.

Page 96 — William C. Burns, quoted in *Five Pioneer Missionaries*, p. 113.

Page 96 — Jonathan Goforth, quoted by Rosalind Goforth, *Jonathan Goforth*, p. 118.

Pages 97-99 — For all quotations relating to Adoniram Judson, see Courtney Anderson, *To the Golden Shore* (repr. Judson Press, 1987), pp. 83, 86, 409, 399.

Pages 99-100 — For all quotations relating to Henry Martyn, see Richard T. France in *Five Pioneer Missionaries*, pp. 245, 248, 252, 253, 297, 301.

Pages 100-102 — For all quotations relating to John Paton, see John D. Legg in *Five Pioneer Missionaries*, pp. 309-310, 338.

Page 103 — The Scriptures cited are Psa. 45:10; Mark 16:15; Matt. 28:19; Luke 10:3.

Page 105 - Robert Murray M'Cheyne, cited from Andrew A. Bonar, ed., *Robert Murray M'Cheyne. Memoir and Remains* (repr. Banner of Truth, 1966), p. 14.

Page 105 — W. E. Sangster, quoted in Leonard Ravenhill, *Why Revival Tarries* (Bethany, 1962), p. 68.

Page 106 — Jonathan Edwards, quoted in the biographical sketch of Edwards by Philip E. Howard, Jr., in *The Life and Diary of David Brainerd*, ed. Jonathan Edwards (Moody, 1949), p. 18.

Page 107 — For William Carey, see Ruth Tucker, *From Jerusalem to Irian Jaya*, p. 115.

Page 108 — David Brown, quoted in *Five Pioneer Missionaries*, p. 280.

Page 108 — Henry Venn, quoted in J. C. Ryle, *Select Sermons*, p. 40.

Page 109 — For the fifteen criteria, see Arnold Dallimore, *Whitefield*, Vol. I, p. 80.

Pages 109-110 — For the Whitefield quotes, see Dallimore, Vol. II, p. 388; Ryle, *Select Sermons*, pp. 39-40; Pollock, *Great Awakening*, p. 246.

Page 111 — John Fletcher, quoted in A. Skevington Wood, *The Burning Heart* (Bethany, 1978), p. 124.

Page 111 — Robert Murray M'Cheyne, *Memoir and Remains*, p. 14.

Page 114 — Nate Krupp, *The Church Triumphant at the End of the Age* (Destiny Image, 1984), p. 208.

Page 117 — Jerome, cited in Jill Haak Adels, *The Wisdom of the Saints* (Oxford, 1987), p. 75.

MISSIONS OPPORTUNITIES!

Has God prompted you to be involved in world missions? Would you like to know how you can help reap the greatest harvest in world history? There are at least three things you can do: *pray, give,* or *go.* Here are some missions organizations that we personally work with and recommend. All of them are worthy of your prayerful and financial support, and they could use solid, committed laborers!

For long-term opportunities in Europe (including
the former Soviet Union), write:
Clark Slone
Cristo e la Risposta (Christ is the Answer)
Sferuzzi Cosimo
Via Cupa del Gesu, 32
47-82100 Benevento
ITALY

For long-term or short-term opportunities in Central
and South America or Russia, write:
Dick Bashta
Global Strategy Missions Association
13855 Plank Road
Baker, LA 70714

To support native workers reaching unreached
tribal villages in India, write:
P. Yesupaddam
Love-N-Care Ministries
c/o Herb Severs
206 Grove Street
Bennington, VT 05201

ICN Ministries has prepared a complete resource catalog of materials by Dr. Michael L. Brown. Included in this catalog are books, audiotapes, videotapes, and self-study courses dealing with:

- Repentance and Revival

- Spiritual Life

- Prayer and Intercession

- Holiness

- Prophetic Ministry

- Divine Healing

- The Church and the Jewish People

- Answering Jewish Objections to Jesus

- Debate and Dialog with Rabbis and Anti-Missionaries

To request our resource catalog, write, call, or fax to:

ICN Ministries
P.O. Box 36157
Pensacola, FL 32506
(850) 458-6424
(850) 458-1828
E-mail: RevivalNow@msn.com

About the Author

Dr. Michael L. Brown is founder and president of ICN Ministries, devoted to taking the message of repentance and revival to Israel, the Church, and the Nations. He has preached throughout the United States and in numerous foreign countries, emphasizing radical discipleship, holy living, and the visitation of the Spirit. His books, articles, and messages have been translated into more than a dozen languages. In 1996, he became part of the ministry team at the Brownsville Revival, holding weekly sessions for leaders and heading up the revival's intensive two-year School of Ministry.

As a Jewish believer in Jesus, Dr. Brown is active in Jewish evangelism and has debated rabbis on radio, TV, and college campuses. He is also a published Old Testament and Semitic scholar, holding a Ph.D. in Near Eastern Languages and Literatures from New York University. In 1997, he was appointed Visiting Professor of Jewish Apologetics at Fuller Theological Seminary of World Mission and has been affiliated with Regent University Divinity School as an Adjunct Professor of Old Testament and Jewish Studies.

Dialogue, Discussion, and Debate:
Dr. Michael L. Brown and the Rabbis

ICN Ministries offers exciting and eye-opening videotapes and audiotapes of Dr. Brown's debates with leading rabbis and anti-missionaries.

These tapes are excellent for edification, education, and outreach. Watch them, listen to them, and give them out!

For further information, contact ICN Ministries, P.O. Box 36157, Pensacola, FL 32506; call (850) 458-6424, fax (850) 458-1828, or E-mail: RevivalNow@msn.com.

In-Depth Self-Study Courses

Choose from three courses specially prepared by Dr. Michael L. Brown:

Answering Jewish Objections to Jesus. This 12-tape series asks hard questions — and provides solid, sound, and scholarly answers. Ideal for all those involved in Jewish outreach and witnessing. Also excellent for those who have been confused by anti-missionaries. The course includes a study guide and texts.

The Messiah in Jewish Tradition. Learn the many and varied Jewish beliefs about the Messiah from the Dead Sea scrolls to the Talmud; from the Bible to Jewish mysticism. A fascinating, firsthand encounter with the ancient and medieval writings. Twelve tapes with textbook and study guide.

I Am the Lord Your Healer. This in-depth, faith-building teaching will help lay solid foundations of the Word in your life. Based on a careful study of the Hebrew and Greek, this comprehensive and practical course can easily be understood by any interested believer. Sixteen tapes, a study guide, and Dr. Brown's full-length study *Israel's Divine Healer* are included.

Available through ICN Ministries, P.O. Box 36157, Pensacola, FL 32506; call (850) 458-6424, fax (850) 458-1828, or E-mail: RevivalNow@msn.com.